A PROVEN PLAY-MAKER'S
RULES OF THE GAME.

Management Myth: "Motivation is the secret to successful management."

Tarkenton's Truth: "A winning performance always beats a winning attitude. Give me action, not motivation."

Management Myth: "For big successes, risk the big play."

Tarkenton's Truth: "Beware the big play: The 80-yard drive is better than the 80-yard pass."

Management Myth: "Superstars can carry the team."

Tarkenton's Truth: "It takes a team to make a superstar."

Management Myth: "Talent always beats experience."

Tarkenton's Truth: "You don't know whether a play works until you run it— get into the arena and play your game. No good decision was ever made in a swivel chair."

PLAYING TO WIN

PLAYING to WIN

Fran Tarkenton's Strategies for Business Success

BY FRAN TARKENTON

BANTAM BOOKS
TORONTO · NEW YORK · LONDON · SYDNEY · AUCKLAND

PLAYING TO WIN:
FRAN TARKENTON'S STRATEGIES FOR BUSINESS SUCCESS

*A Bantam Book / published by arrangement with
Harper & Row, Publishers, Inc.*

PRINTING HISTORY

Harper & Row edition published April 1984

*Appeared as a 3-part serialization
in the New York Post, Fall 1984*

Bantam edition / May 1985

ISBN 0-553-25079-5

Published simultaneously in the United States and Canada

*Bantam Books are published by Bantam Books, Inc. Its trade-
mark, consisting of the words "Bantam Books" and the por-
trayal of a rooster, is Registered in U.S. Patent and Trademark
Office and in other countries. Marca Registrada. Bantam
Books, Inc., 666 Fifth Avenue, New York, New York 10103.*

PRINTED IN THE UNITED STATES OF AMERICA

H   0 9 8 7 6 5 4 3 2 1

CONTENTS

CONTENTS

ACKNOWLEDGMENTS

Many people have contributed over the years to my understanding of the winning strategies in business and sports. But none has been so constantly a partner in my enterprises as Tom Joiner, my fraternity brother, attorney and the president of Tarkenton Productivity Group, Inc. As this book shows, so many outstanding American business leaders have given me the benefit of their experience that it would be hopeless to try to name them all. Yet I would like to acknowledge the one who made contact with all the others possible when he gave a young quarterback-turned-businessman his very first consulting account: Roger Milliken, chairman of Milliken & Company in Spartanburg, South Carolina.

As you will also find out in this book, I

learned some of the most important lessons about management from my many years on the playing fields of the Minnesota Vikings. I owe a major debt to my teammates during those great years and particularly to one of the best managers I have ever met, Coach Bud Grant.

With all that, this book would never have made it to print without the tireless exertions of my secretary, Sharon Brown, and my boyhood friend, journalist Peter Ross Range.

PLAYING
to
WIN

INTRODUCTION

Running a business is a lot like quarterbacking a football team. I know. During eighteen hard-scrambling years with the Minnesota Vikings and the New York Giants, I managed dozens of oversized madmen in shoulder pads feverishly trying to put points on a scoreboard. My job was getting high performance out of these talented, single-minded people who—as one of them told me—didn't have to punch in, but always punched out. I led hundreds of tense business meetings—kindly known as huddles—to improve our bottom line: our score. I learned ways to confront the onrush of competitive forces: usually 250-pound tackles, ends and linebackers.

And for my own survival, I had to do some

quick strategic planning, which is why I became known as a "scrambler." I now feel a little like a former Buffalo Bills quarterback, Congressman Jack Kemp, who said, "Pro football gave me a good sense of perspective to enter politics—I'd already been booed, cheered, cut, sold, traded, and hung in effigy."

Like football, business is a game—but it is the game where the clock never stops and the score can change every day. Today, I find business an even more exciting game than football, because the stakes are higher and the rewards greater.

The goal of any organization or any team is to win, to beat your own record, to turn a profit. Yet, one of the things I discovered in my eighteen years in the pros and nearly that many in business is that businessmen today are living on myths. Many of these myths are based on sports but have nothing to do with the reality of either the gridiron or the boardroom. These myths are destructive; they rob you of success and keep you from delivering a winning performance.

So... here's the book I *didn't* write. It contains all the rules I *don't* believe in—either on the playing field or in the boardroom:

1. A manager's job is to think, not to play
2. Motivation is the secret to successful management
3. People work mainly for money

4. One-minute praisings—the most praise-worthy thing to do
5. One-minute reprimands—put people in their place
6. Managers should manage themselves
7. Macho makes the man a manager
8. Winners don't make mistakes
9. A winner never quits
10. For big successes, risk the Big Play
11. Superstars can carry the team
12. Listen to the Monday-morning quarter-backs
13. "Talent always beats experience"
14. One-sided deals leave you sitting pretty
15. A smart leader has all the answers
16. Always play as if you are ahead
17. Hard work ensures success
18. To come out ahead, beware the compe-tition
19. Second always finishes behind first

None of this is true in my opinion. What I've learned about business from sports is that the key to both is people—and a winning attitude that you can create to psych up yourself and others. No quarterback can be successful unless he's confident and capable of bringing the ten other men on his offensive team together with all their energy and spirit. The moment the football is snapped, the quarterback needs all the skills of *involvement, goal-setting, feedback* and *reinforce-ment*—the same ones that work in business.

You've probably never heard a football player use that kind of "psychological" language before to describe the business of running a team. Well, I didn't know those words either—I didn't even know the *concepts*—until I had already thrown a lot of balls and run a lot of plays. Then I realized that the real game was in keeping everyone going. The other game—the one that the stats show—was just the result of playing the mental game superbly.

I was born the son of a preacherman and sometimes it shows. They say the chief impulse that motivates a minister of the Gospel is a desire to spread the good news. Well, I have a bit of that impulse in me, too. And I have been going around the United States for years, even before I retired from football, telling folks what I have learned about success and leadership from my many years in football and almost that many in business.

In 1971, while I was still with the Giants, I found that after I became a businessman, I became a better quarterback. I learned how to manage human resources better. I founded my own management consulting business. Tarkenton & Company (now Tarkenton Productivity Group, Inc.) has by now worked with some three hundred companies all over the country—and abroad. We have brought our techniques of performance evaluation and productivity to over 250,000 people—from line workers to top management. From doing this, I feel I've learned something

about what makes people care about their jobs
and what raises their performance to star quality.

As chairman of Tarkenton Productivity
Group, Inc., I spend a great deal of time talking
to business groups around the country. I come
into contact with chief executive officers from
every kind of company: with a financial services
wizard such as James D. Robinson, chairman of
American Express; with textiles mogul Roger
Milliken; and with electronics giant Harry Gray,
chairman of United Technologies Corporation.
As Jimmy Robinson once said to me, "Fran, I
think you know more CEO's than anyone else in
the country."

In fact, what I've learned about business
and productivity did not come from books—it
came from people, people in football and in
business. Whatever smarts I have in this business are street smarts. I believe in *learning by
listening!* Whenever I'm around successful businessmen, I *learn.* I ask a million questions. I
milk people dry. I take advantage of every plane
ride and luncheon meeting and golf match. I
know how to get people talking: *by sincerely
asking for their help.* People love to help—but
you have to ask.

So I've been very lucky. I've spent half a
lifetime in a sport that requires teamwork, high
morale, a winning spirit and the constant search
for better performance. *I learned to learn*—and
was in fact learning the art of quarterbacking *at
a faster rate* in my last year in the pro game than

in my first. As a quarterback, I had benefit of special training in how to manage human resources into a successful and productive unit, even though I didn't have the greatest arm or the fleetest feet in the trade. *Just like businessmen looking at the bottom line, the offensive team of the Minnesota Vikings had to put points on the board!* I was the field manager of this enterprise.

I even learned by staying abreast of what was going on in the front office of my football teams. In fact, during all those years on the playing field, *I was really just a businessman masquerading as a football player.*

My spreading the news about football and management is not good for anything, of course, unless you, the receiver, do something with it. It is like passing the football: it does no good for me to shoot a perfect spiral 25 yards downfield if there is no one there to catch it. *I can't catch my own passes.* My message won't help anybody if it only gets you excited for a couple of days before you get caught up again in your old routines.

This is not a scientific book that will answer all your questions about management or the business of your life. But it is a practical, action-oriented guide to survival and success in a confusing and challenging world. It is practical and action-oriented because that is the way I learned the lessons myself: by trying them out.

So here's the book I did write.

It contains the rules that worked for me on the

football field and the ones that I have found most applicable to the business world. They explode the myths that have been lifted from the Vince Lombardi lore and point the way toward greater productivity, higher performance and new levels of personal satisfaction. For me, they are the secrets to attaining a winning edge—in football and in business.

1.

MYTH: *A Manager's Job Is to Think, Not to Play*

Many managers in America today have fallen into what I call the press-box syndrome. They spend their lives ruminating at desks and living through endless meetings. They are engulfed in reports, and spend more time thinking and observing than doing. They tend to isolate themselves from the real world of business around them. They are not in the arena, playing the game. If a football player did that, he would soon be on the bus back to mama.

Yet, the truth is: *You don't know whether a play works if you don't run it.* On the blackboard or in the playbook, every play looks perfect. On paper, you score every time. But sometimes when you take a play out on the practice field, you can try it out all day long and find out it stinks.

In the business world, this means that if you always wait until the right time or the good times to start an enterprise or a new project, you'll wait all your life.

So the corollary to the first rule is: *It's okay to make mistakes*. In fact, it is a good thing to make mistakes, because this means *you are stretching* and working your way through a process of elimination—eliminating all the *wrong* solutions. Each wrong step thus brings you that much closer to the right one and teaches you something at the same time.

Jerry Burns, my offensive coach when I was with the Minnesota Vikings, used to say, "You can get the plays off the back of a Wheaties cereal box, boys. *But it's up to you to make 'em work.*"

Coach Burns, besides being the funniest man I've ever known, was strictly action-oriented. Whenever one of us would raise his hand in a team meeting and ask, "What do we do if their defense does such-and-such?" old Burnsie would always answer, "Whatever it takes, boys." That was his philosophy: *You do whatever it takes to win*. If that means breaking with conventional wisdom and past practices, then so be it.

That's why I became a scrambler—a quarterback who does not stay in the "passing pocket" 7 yards behind the center on every passing play. A scrambler becomes a "mobile" quarterback, able to save plays and frustrate the defense by running around the backfield until he finds one of his receivers open. Sometimes he even runs with the ball himself. Sometimes he also gets tackled behind the line of scrimmage for a big loss, but that is *the risk you must be willing to take*.

Scrambling is an emergency solution to pressure. It is like the businessman's knowing how to change his product line in mid-market. The ultimate scramble, I suppose, is today's Japanese economic miracle. They turned the ultimate disaster—defeat in war—into the springboard for the greatest business success story in the country's history.

Being a "scrambler" was a severe break with the tradition of the great quarterbacks: Y. A. Tittle, Sammy Baugh, Otto Graham, John Unitas and my own first coach, the late Norm Van Brocklin. These men were aghast that I was running out of the pocket. Van Brocklin used to say about me: "He'll win some games that way that he shouldn't, but he'll always lose some that he shouldn't."

That was like the doomsayers who predicted I would never make it at all in the National Football League because I was relatively small (only 6 feet tall and 190 pounds) and weak of arm. Even my own coach in my All-America year at the University of Georgia, Wally Butts, said that. By traditional pro standards, he was right.

But that's just it: I am not bound by tradition, in sports or in business. *If you let the past dictate the future, you will never go anywhere*. What a dull life it would be if you could see your whole life mapped out in front of you just by looking backward. It reminds me of the player who lost a coaching job because he didn't have the experience. His point was that the Pilgrims didn't have any experience when they landed here. If experience was that important, would we ever have had anybody landing on the moon?

I live by the concept of "feed forward," which means you should rehearse any future plays you're considering in your mind. Your only limitation is the script in your head and the fear in your heart. Because I did not live by feedback *alone* (the lessons of the past), I could become a scrambler.

Because of the restraints of tradition, nobody had successfully tried scrambling before, so I had to pioneer it. Of course, it is not something I thought up and planned out. It was my natural reaction to some 270-pound tackle thundering down on me at full gallop. Being smaller, slower, and weaker in the throwing department than a pro quarterback is supposed to be, *I had to come up with something that worked!* For me, scrambling worked. I may have been small, but I agreed with the dictum of California coach Pappy Waldorf: "Good players win games for you, not big players."

Scrambling was simply my way of dealing with a *productivity problem on the football field.* While Van Brocklin and the others were talking about the "proven" virtue of staying in the passing pocket (and letting those big guys crush you in a heap occasionally), I was always remembering one of the first lessons I learned from Weyman Sellers, my high school coach in Athens, Georgia: "The quarterback's job is to gain yardage and score points." Falling in a heap on the ground just did not seem the best way to reach those goals. I wanted a more productive way to deal with a broken block or a defensive blitz. So I scrambled.

By the time I retired from football eighteen years after Van Brocklin said I shouldn't scramble, I had broken and far surpassed all passing records in the history of the pro game, including most touchdown passes (342), most pass completions (3,686) and most yards gained passing (47,003).

So my philosophy is, When in doubt, *do something!* I agree with the approach of J. Peter Grace, chairman of W. R. Grace & Co. Peter once compared his corporate success to the way he made himself into a top college ice hockey player by going out alone to work on "practical hockey . . . night after night." He added, "It's the same way in business. Only something you start working on *today* will pay off in five years."

My whole life has been directed toward action. Whenever somebody presented me with a problem, I have always gone out and started working on it right away. I don't spend too much time theorizing or analyzing. I just start trying to *do something* about it. I probably do it wrong the first five or six times, but on the seventh try, I get it right. The main thing is, to get to that right solution, *you gotta get moving right now!*

You win by trying, not by standing around!

The trend in recent years has been to take a more contemplative, analytical approach to problem-solving. Our celebrated business and management schools teach a highly abstracted approach to management of organizations and people. Theirs is a game of numbers and percentiles. It is fashionable to put down the *do something* approach with a twist on the old joke, "Don't just stand there—do something!" This philosophy believes that much damage has been wrought by those who plunged unthinkingly ahead, acting only on gut instinct instead of moving with a careful plan.

I believe the trouble this country is in today stems from too much analyzing and too little action, too many meetings and not enough hands-on practice. Harry Gray, chairman of the $14 billion United Technologies Corporation, is a real action-oriented, no-nonsense manager. He says, "ninety-eight percent of the talk goes to two percent of the problem. . . . At your next meeting remove the chairs, empty the carafes, turn the thermostat down to fifty-five. A stand-up meeting could be a standout."

One of the consequences of analysis without action is a collective timidity in our business community. The Japanese did not attain their extraordinary market shares in cars, electronics and other fields by playing a conservative game.

They invested time, money and human resources, took serious risks and pulled themselves up by their wooden sandals from total defeat in war.

In America, meanwhile, we seem to have gotten so comfortable in our old boots—and our old ways—that we don't even know where the bootstraps are anymore.

In sports, it is a matter of being willing to bang your shins and bloody your nose once in a while. All the game plans in the world aren't worth anything if they stay in the playbook. Sooner or later, you have to get into the arena and play the game.

It is just the same in business. Henry Ford did not fill the roads of America with all-black Model T's just by thinking about it. He had to go out one day and *make it happen*.

The best thing you can do is to get yourself tired of all the talk and excuses about *why something can't be done*. You've got to want to *do something*. You've got to take an action approach. Legendary Alabama coach Bear Bryant generated such a feeling by posting a sign in the players' locker room: "Cause something to happen." That's my philosophy: *Make it happen*.

FACT: *When all is said and done, more is said than done.* **Make it happen!**

2.

MYTH: *Motivation Is the Secret to Successful Management*

In my book, motivation is the biggest myth of all. It does nothing more than raise the adrenalin— temporarily—which might work while you're kicking the ball. But business, remember, is the game where the clock never stops. Sure, you want your team members to play every day as if they were planting the flag on Iwo Jima, but you won't motivate them to do it.

That's why, when people ask me how to get "a winning attitude," I tell them there is no such thing as a winning attitude. There is only *a winning performance.*

What is an attitude? Is it something we can see, feel or measure? Is it some vague state of mind rattling around inside a person? Well, yes,

I suppose the psychologists would say so. But as a quarterback or a manager, that is not something I can realistically deal with. All I can deal with is what the human body can do when chased by a bigger human body.

The same thing applies to the rather elusive term "motivation." Frankly, I don't know what that is. I can't see it, feel it or measure it. What I can see and feel and measure, however, is *performance*. Once when Bum Phillips was comparing Earl Campbell and George Rogers, he said, "Rogers *sees* daylight, Campbell *makes* daylight." To me, Campbell's work was the more crucial.

Let me put it more directly: If one of my linemen was making consistently good blocks, I considered him to be "motivated." As far as I was concerned, he had a "winning attitude." What he really had, of course, was real and measurable *good performance*.

When you're out there 6 points behind with third and ten and only thirty seconds left on the clock, you aren't looking for that undefined thing called a good attitude, you're looking for performance. The real question is, "Can this man get it done?" Better still, *will* he get it done?

I don't care if a man picks his nose or hates my face or dresses ugly, if he is the right guard who can block those pass rushers on that critical play, he is giving me a winning performance, which *gives me a chance to win, too*. To me, a winning performance *is* a winning attitude.

Charlie Pell, Clemson football coach, said it best. Above all, he demanded attitude coupled with action from his players. "I want them to think as positively as the eighty-five-year-old man who married a twenty-five-year-old woman and ordered a five-bedroom house near an elementary school." If you play as determinedly as that old man, nothing can keep you from winning.

The motivated guy may seem the cheeriest, most likable and best-thing-for-the-company soul. But what good is he really? I have teamed up with many players I did not like. I didn't want to socialize with them or go out and be seen in public with them. On any football team, you have maybe four or five guys who are your friends. Then there are a bunch of others who you think are okay. And finally there is another group that you consider, quite frankly, assholes. No matter what kind of a team *you* are now playing on—in business or in sports—I think you know what I mean.

Now, who in these groups has the "winning attitude?" The guy who never misses practice, works hard and yet can't quite produce the winning performance; or the lazy troublemaker who somehow always delivers when it counts? He might not have liked me, the coach, the team or even the game of football. But if he knocked the defensive guy on his ass, that was a winning performance. This is a slightly exaggerated situation, but I would have to say the bad guy with the winning performance is the one with the "right" attitude here. Attitude and performance go hand in hand.

The same thing happens in business. You have some people who are always there, who speak to you and smile every day, display every intention of doing their best, but somehow just don't make those sales. And the person you like least may in his own way be getting the job done better. This is not a brief for unscrupulousness or the philosophy that "nice guys finish last." It is simply my observation that attitude and performance have to be one and the same.

I believe a winning attitude combined with performance springs from the kind of management you have. I have seen great football players turned mediocre by mediocre organizations. Lousy management can destroy a winning attitude.

I have always had a "winning attitude" —which is just another way of saying I had my share of wins and so I expected to win. It was more a response to a learned behavior: winning. And I will admit I was extremely lucky in this regard because I was successful at sports.

What produces a winning performance in business or sports is a solid organization that the players or employees can believe in. And it starts at the top. If you don't believe in the leaders of your organization, how can you truly believe in the organization? There must be serious people at the top who sincerely believe in the product, who give good direction and feedback, who send out the right vibes and hire the right supervisors, managers or coaches.

Perhaps the key quality of all is consistency. The members of your business or sports team have to know what is going on, know what they can expect for themselves and their teammates and not be blindsided for reporting truthfully when something is going wrong. (The day your players start telling you what they *think* you want to hear is the day you know you're in trouble.) If your players know you are consistent and your organization is without significant cracks, they will go to the wall for you. This is a far greater motivator than Knute Rockne speeches or sales contests with trips to Hawaii as prizes. This is what makes football teams such as the Miami Dolphins, Dallas Cowboys and Minnesota Vikings consistent and perennial winners: they have solid, dependable management. And the opposite is what has doomed the New Orleans Saints and the Detroit Lions to erratic performance. There is terrible disruption in their management. Coaches come and go. Ownership changes. It is impossible for strong leadership to emerge.

Furthermore, management cannot win that does not believe in itself or in its product. If you are going to sell apple pies, you have to believe you are producing the best apple pie around. Or the best tractor. Or the best football team. *One of the first steps to a winning performance is believing in what you are doing.* That principle cannot be compromised for money, glory, ego, social recognition or anything else. If you don't believe in what you are doing or selling, you are just bullshitting yourself. And that is the beginning of a losing attitude/performance.

In the business world, people have often thought of me as a "motivational" speaker. It is true that I am very enthusiastic about everything I do and sometimes that excitement seems to catch on with the people I am speaking to. At least they are nodding their heads and smiling a lot when I tell some of my stories about the lessons I have learned from football and business. And it is true that early in my career, right out of college, I used to make a lot of win-one-for-the-Gipper speeches.

But after I got into business and began speaking to audiences in the higher-stakes world of corporate America, I began to notice some disturbing things. I could go into a large corporate convention and make drum-thumping speeches that had people on their feet and clapping their hands. But a year later, I would be invited back to make that same speech again to that same company, and I found out their performance and productivity had not really changed that much—which is why they wanted me back.

I once made a series of nearly one hundred speeches for one of America's greatest companies, IBM. Suddenly one day it dawned on me that I was not having any real-world effect on the lives or performances of the salesmen I was speaking to. I could get them all charged up for a day or two, but when they got back out into the field and had the first few doors slammed in their faces, they were thinking, "Okay, where is Tarkenton now?" Tarkenton was off somewhere else to give the next motivational speech and entertain the troops at their annual sales meeting.

This Knute Rockne approach has contributed to the myth in business that the way to get higher performance out of people is through pep talks or by a lot of yelling and screaming. This latter method is also part of the great Vince Lombardi mythology.

I believe Lombardi has been badly misunderstood. We have focused too much on the myth that he said, "winning is the only thing." He didn't, in fact. We have all heard stories such as the one from the great Green Bay tackle Forrest Gregg, who once said, "Lombardi treats us all alike—like dogs." But from talking with many other men who played on Lombardi's teams, and from my own experience playing for him in one Pro Bowl, I have learned there was more to his success than this alone.

For one thing, Lombardi was a very organized, disciplined person. He was a good example to his players. He exhibited many of the qualities that were important to the success of his players: self-discipline, dedicated and consistent efforts toward a goal, the ability to sacrifice immediate gratification for a greater achievement. He was also a very clear thinker. Few people realize that he ran only eight or ten plays on the offense. But the plays were run out of different formations and always very cleanly executed. Like all the great teachers, he had the job of the football player broken down into simple tasks that each man could master. And he was consistent—even with his emotional outbursts, players knew what to expect. Consistency is a key part of leadership.

More important, Lombardi delegated authority. Like Coach Bud Grant of the Vikings, he recognized that *he couldn't do everything!* Too many managers believe they have to be everywhere and know everything. Not Lombardi: He chose the best experts he could find as his assistant coaches and let them be his field specialists.

I think these qualities had more to do with Lombardi's famous success as a coach than the infamous tirades we have heard about. In fact, it has been my experience that the yellers and the screamers are not the coaches who win. Neither Bud Grant nor Tom Landry nor Don Shula— three of the winningest coaches in modern football—do it that way.

So when I went out to give "motivational" speeches, I began thinking about what was going on. I could get men so enthusiastic at these banquets that they wanted to go out and make some sales calls right after dessert. But when it came to the actual business of doing it a few days later, I had not given them any practical tools to work with. They were up the proverbial creek with a lot of enthusiasm but no paddle.

So I decided to quit giving high-powered pep talks. Instead, I began to equip the people who came to listen to me with the tools for successful performance—the things they would need when they got away from the sales conventions and had to get back into the trenches of real-world business.

I've always remembered what Hank Stram, former NFL coach, had to say about performance: "Yesterday is a canceled check, today is cash on the line, tomorrow is a promissory note." That's how I feel about doing well at business. Your cash on the line—that daily performance—is all that should matter. Motivation is as good as a promissory note. Try to get yourself a cup of coffee with one of those.

FACT: *A winning performance always beats a winning attitude. Give me action, not motivation.*

3.

MYTH: *People Work Mainly for Money*

People don't win the Super Bowl because they are working for money. If they did, the highest-paid team in the league should win it every year.

Most people don't work strictly for money. In case you think that's a misprint, let me say it this way: Your work means the most to you not on the day of your new raise but when you've accomplished something besides good sales and more money. Your performance isn't a function of your salary, but your salary should be a function of your performance.

Of course, you won't put in time without getting paid. But money alone won't keep you working well and hard once you show up. You can buy someone's time, but not his soul. Or his performance.

Chuck Tanner, major league baseball manager, put it this way: "You can have money stacked to the ceiling, but the size of your funeral is still going to depend on the weather." That's also true of the commitment you bring to work. What keeps you working is *involvement*. What gets you involved is accountability. And what keeps people accountable is the scoreboard. It works in football and the same in business. Let me tell you why.

One of the most gratifying things in sports is the scoreboard. In football and basketball, you look up over the arena and you know exactly how you stand. In golf, you carry the scorecard in your pocket; in tennis it's in your head or on the umpire's pad. Leads can change, but good effort (and a little luck) is instantly rewarded with points on the board. When you are behind, you are therefore driven to catch up; when ahead, to hold on. And when time runs out—or the final ball is hit—everybody knows who won and who lost.

How do we keep score in business? After all, business is the game where the clock never stops and the score can change every day. There is no great scoreboard in the sky that you can look up to during a lunchtime huddle or at the end of the day and know whether you're winning or losing. In manufacturing and sales, very few people can leave at the end of the week and say, "I won" or "I lost." *They just don't know*.

And yet we all like to know how we're doing. I would hate to have to play in a sport with no score-keeping system. It is difficult to stay excited during a game if you don't know who is winning. During my playing years, that big scoreboard was a pretty reinforcing thing to those of us down on the football field.

And I think a lot of people in America see business as a game. I even agree with Ted Turner, the rough-riding Atlanta sportsman and television mogul, who once compared running a traditional business to operating his baseball team, the Atlanta Braves.

"To me, business is a game," he said. "It's like a poker game: you're playing for chips, but the most fun is the game. You keep score with dollars, to a degree. But it's like there are two kinds of points. Money is like hits in a baseball game. They're great, but the runs are what really count. And the runs are just being successful and having a good time. It takes a lot of hits to win a game. You can have more hits than the other team and still lose the game. The dollars are one way of keeping score, but not the primary way."

If dollars are not the primary way of keeping score in business, what is? Sure, dollars are one way of measuring your success in your business. When your salary goes up, you feel you've made progress. You're successfully climbing the corporate ladder. When sales are up, everybody feels good. But one of the most important things I have discovered, both as a professional athlete and as a businessman, is that people don't work for money: they work for satisfaction, for community, for participation, for a sense of productivity.

I first discovered this when I started making a lot of money in football. My salary with the New York Giants was about $50,000, and during my five years there it rose into six figures. But a funny thing happened: my salary went up, but I played some of my worst football in my last years with the Giants, even though I was more experienced, knew more about strategy and was more confident simply because I was *making a lot more money*. The point here is that *making more money did not make me perform better*. My performance improved markedly when I was traded back to the Minnesota Vikings—but that had everything to do with the quality of the organization, not with my salary, which remained the same.

It's the same with one of the greatest athletes of our time: Reggie Jackson. I've admired Reggie's career for a long time, from his days with the Oakland A's to the New York Yankees and then back to the California Angels. During all those years, Reggie's salary made meteoric leaps. But I noticed that Reggie's performance didn't *double* every time his salary did. Reggie was great at Oakland, great at New York, and great again at California. Reggie's salary had nothing to do with how well he played the game. He was "Mr. October" before he made the big bucks. He won play-off games simply because he wanted to win. It was love of the game, love of the limelight, dislike for George Steinbrenner— whatever put a smile on Reggie's face and drew that superior performance out of him; not his salary. On the contrary, *salary was a function of performance, not the other way around.*

I never made anything like the money Reggie makes as an athlete. Yet I was trying just as hard for quarterbacking perfection as Reggie does for hitting greatness. He will go down as the man who hit three home runs in a single World Series game and I will stay in the record books for quite a while as the man with the most passes, touchdowns and aerial yardage.

We were both driven by the same impulses, but they had nothing to do with the desire for money. This is true of people working at any level. Of course, most people will tell you they are working to support themselves and their families. But our training projects in plants all over the country have shown us that performance increases not when you give people more money, but when they are offered the chance for visible, measurable satisfaction.

Perhaps the best proof that money alone won't enhance productivity lies in the American automobile industry. It fell into its worst slump during the very period that workers' salaries were rising the most. When the industry began concentrating more on the workers' roles and quality circles, productivity increased even though some labor groups took pay cuts. Job satisfaction seems to matter more than the tangible rewards of cash and benefits.

The bottom line is that people work for the score; they work to win, to beat their own records. Their success breeds success. The doffer in a textile mill who is suddenly producing over 200 pounds of yarn per hour instead of 140 or 150 is performing better just for the sake of performing better—because it feels so good. And it often comes about just because someone bothers to ask the doffer about his performance and pay attention to how well he does. He's then working for approval and has a score-keeping system (pounds of yarn per hour) to measure himself by. That's when doffing becomes a game. "Can I beat yesterday's performance?" he may ask himself in the middle of the shift when he notices he has already reached 180 pounds per hour. "What happens if I cut short my coffee break a few minutes?" The doffer has now become self-motivated and is like the quarterback whose adrenalin level varies according to the numbers he sees on the scoreboard.

Now, where does money come into this score-keeping system? It is just like the example of Reggie Jackson. This doffer's salary may go up as a function of increased performance—and it should. A 1983 poll showed that half of American workers see no relationship between how hard they work and how much they get paid. More than 60 percent said they wanted their jobs tied to performance.

But when we have studied cases where management tried to raise performance by raising pay *first,* we have invariably found that it doesn't work. *Productivity is not a function of salary; salary must be a function of productivity.*

The corollary to this rule is: *You can't buy performance—you've got to manage performance.*

FACT: *Performance is not a function of salary; salary is a function of performance.*

4.

MYTH: *One-Minute Praisings—The Most Praiseworthy Thing to Do*

No way!

You and I may want to improve our performance. We want raises and "attaboys" and an office that is truly topside of the rockpile. And, yes, we're running hard all the time just to see the score change and get our daily feedback. But what are we fed instead? Programs designed to give us "job satisfaction" and one-minute pep talks. Can you imagine any athlete succeeding from nothing more than pats on the fanny? What we really need is more attention to what we're doing. When I perform well, I want to know it. I want to know how and why my performance was good—and how it can be better. Being a happy player doesn't necessarily make me a better player. The opposite is true: being a better player makes me a happier player.

Managing performance means giving feedback and reinforcement—lots of it, in very specific terms and often. For me, the ultimate form of feedback has always been the scoreboard. In business, you create a scoreboard not so different from the ones in sports: a graph used to chart your own or your employees' performance and production. And it works. Not just in keeping score, but in improving the score. People actually improve their performance just because someone pays attention—often for the first time— to what they're doing. Years ago an experiment showed that people improved their performance when factory lighting was turned *up*, and improved again when it was turned *down*. But productivity remained steady or declined when the lighting was left alone, because people felt they weren't getting any attention. Most of the time I'll increase my productivity *if I know someone cares*.

Andrew S. Grove, president of Intel Corporation, the California semiconductor manufacturer, uses a scoreboard technique in his business. "For years, the performance of the Intel facilities maintenance group, which is responsible for keeping our buildings clean and in good shape, was mediocre; and no amount of pressure or inducement seemed to do any good. We then initiated a program in which each building's upkeep was periodically scored by a resident senior manager, dubbed a 'building czar.' The score was then compared with those given the other buildings. The condition of all of them dramatically improved almost immediately. Nothing else was done; people did not get more money or other rewards. What they did get was an arena of competition."

My style of business scoreboard is based on a procedure called P.R.I.C.E. Think of it as the price you must pay if you want to win. Each letter in P.R.I.C.E. stands for a step to take to create a winning performance for yourself and for your employees. Unlike the zillion management theories floating around the landscape— management by objective, management grids, transactional analysis, theories X, Y and Z—with a lot of ideas but few guides for concrete action— P.R.I.C.E. is a concrete, practical way of beating the odds against you. Here is what the initials stand for:

P = *Pinpoint* any measurable performance of yours that needs to be changed.

R = *Record* the performance on a chart for everyone to see just as he'd track a scoreboard.

I = *Identify* the results of the performance: how much money or time is lost as a result of inattention or a job poorly done; then *intervene* to modify the performance.

C = *Change* the *consequences* of that behavior, give reinforcement and performance feed-

back in the form of praise and recognition
and with graphs and non-money rewards.

E = *Evaluate* the changes in job performance,
continue to review yourself or your employees and modify the consequences based on
the direction of progress.

We've tested P.R.I.C.E. at Tarkenton Productivity Group over a dozen years of consulting
in a variety of manufacturing, sales and service
organizations, with excellent results. What makes
it good is that *it works*.

As a quarterback, I was always searching
for ways to achieve the winning edge. In football,
whenever we do something right, it goes straight
into our records. But in most companies, good
performers don't get much attention (according
to *Boardroom Reports*). Usually, the way to get
reaction from a boss or a coach is *not to perform*.
Managers spend most of their time seeking out
problems, not praising. The beauty of determin-
ing everybody's P.R.I.C.E.—your own included—
is that everybody's performance improves, both
the benchwarmer's *and* the star's.

That's where *pinpointing* behavior becomes
so important. Focus on one step in the process
of doing something that can be observed and
measured. You cannot measure a "bad attitude,"
but you *can* measure how many times you growl
(or make any negative remark) at your colleagues during the day. Doing "poor work" is
not measurable; a certain number of errors per

page in secretarial typing is. Spending "too much time" untangling a spinning frame in a textile mill is not a clear measurement; counting the frequency of misplaced bobbins on the frame is.

You set up your scoreboard by listing these pinpointed behaviors, which are simply things you do, not the effects of what you do. For example, sales won are the outcome of calls made. A completed pass is the result of good footwork, a quick reading of the defense and a smooth release of the ball. It's important to pinpoint accurately the behavior that you want changed to solve a problem, not simply to state the problem itself.

In devising my business scoreboard, I follow the "Dead Man's Rule," which luckily means you are responsible only for actions you are alive to engage in. You can forget about the rest. If your department has an absenteeism problem, you should focus on *attendance* rather than absenteeism. (Even a dead man is absent.) This means you concentrate on praising (reinforcing) what the person does right (coming to work) rather than criticizing what he does wrong (being absent).

Next comes the *record* phase of the scoreboard. One of our clients recognized that some of his employees thought he was "unfriendly," that he wasn't reinforcing their work often enough. The pressures of his job often provoked him to chew people out and to criticize their mistakes. He pinpointed his growling at staff members as the behavior that had to be changed. He then asked his secretary, who sat within earshot of his desk, to mark down every time he made negative or positive remarks over a six-day period, but not to show him the results until the end of the week. Using graph paper and marks to show his daily changes, the manager got a baseline against which to compare his later behavior.

The *identify/intervention* phase came when the secretary gave him the chart at the end of the first week. He was embarrassed to see that he had made more negative than positive comments every day, including one day where the ratio of bad to good was twelve to one.

For the next three weeks, this manager kept the chart in his desk and made his own record of his positive and negative remarks. He was now actively participating and confronted with an ongoing, daily scoreboard on his behavior, noting any *change/consequences* that resulted. From the very first day, his positive remarks began outnumbering the negative ones so that he had reversed the twelve to one ratio by the seventeenth day.

And just as a traditional scoreboard focuses on points and winnings, often the only intervention that workers need is having their performance called to their attention, then being reinforced for *positive* results. One of the country's largest record-producing companies pinpointed a problem at the end stage of the manufacturing process. The department in charge of enclosing the albums in their final plastic wrapping was falling behind the pace of the rest of the plant. Finished records were stacking up in the department faster than the shrink-wrap operators could prepare them for shipment. Production was below engineered standards.

The first thing the department foreman did was to establish a baseline of performance. He kept records over the course of three months. They showed that each of the eight operators in the department was wrapping an average of 5,991 records per day.

For the intervention stage, the foreman posted both individual and group charts within the department. Each operator could measure himself (keep score!) against his co-workers every day, as well as see the department's aggregate total and individual average performance per day. The stated goal was to achieve a higher average performance *across the board*. This reinforced individual *as well as* group performance. The foreman reinforced the operators with personal praise as their performance increased. For especially dramatic improvement, he also wrote the operator a memo of commendation. As a result, the department's productivity during the following year rose by fully 27 percent, to an average of 7,662 records wrapped per person per day.

The program was so successful that the foreman instituted similar methods in another department at an earlier stage of production, the one where the records were inserted into their jackets. This seems to have had a stimulating effect on the record-wrapping department, because in the next year it averaged 8,789 units wrapped per person per day—fully 46 percent above the original baseline.

By this time, the operators in the department were no longer working simply to "improve the department standard," but began setting their own goals based on previous individual and departmental records. This meant that the foreman's personal reinforcement gradually became less important; the operators had in effect developed their own built-in systems of reinforcement by trying to set new records.

Just as in sports, scorekeeping led to goal-setting, which led to record-breaking. By establishing a scoreboard that initially showed the home team losing vis-à-vis the other departments, the players became concerned about their performance. But the scoreboard did something even more important: it established *accountability*. Before the scorekeeping started, workers may have been vaguely aware that too many albums were piling up, but no one considered this his personal problem in the greater scheme of things. No one could relate personal performance to team performance and profitability. Suddenly, everyone felt responsible for what was now a noticeable problem.

The same thing will work in sales. You may find your monthly and weekly sales rate dropping off without understanding why. That's when it is time to *go back to basics*. Either you or one of your colleagues should create some baseline data by charting your behaviors over a week or more. How many phone calls per day are you making to old or prospective clients? How many times per day do you check the newspaper or trade literature for possible leads on *new* prospects, clients or contacts? How many personal face-to-face sales calls are you making per week? How many times per week are you asking for an account?

After one or two weeks, tally these numbers on a chart. Then set objectives that you can reasonably meet for gradually increasing the frequency of each of these behaviors. Forget about sales—they are the *result*—and focus on the *behaviors*: phone calls, prospecting, sales calls and asking for accounts. After reaching your new goals over a full week, set a new level of attainable objectives. Raise your performance in each of these *categories for winning*, and the outcome—increased sales—will take care of itself.

FACT: *Give your people a scoreboard: They need to know whether they are winning or losing.*

5.

MYTH: *One-Minute Reprimands—Put People in Their Place*

"A lot of managers focus on weaknesses. And we all have them. I think that's a fundamental mistake. *You have to look at the beauty spots*. We all have those, too." So says my buddy Donald Keough, president of the terrifically successful Coca-Cola Company.

"When you do that, and let the person sense it," says Don, "then you get all the best that's in them. And they're not demeaned or destroyed by your constantly reaching in to find their weaknesses."

I agree. *Feedback* and *reinforcement* are two simple approaches you probably use in your personal life all the time, but I'll bet you overlook them in business dealings just as I once did in sports. Feedback lets someone know how you are reacting to his behavior. It tells him what effects his behavior is having on his performance and on the people around him. I don't know I am working too slowly on a project if someone doesn't tell me. I wouldn't know I was handing off the football too low on the beltline if my fullback didn't tell me. That's feedback.

Reinforcement goes a step farther. Reinforcement is a way of trying to increase or decrease a certain behavior. When you spank a baby for throwing his dinner on the floor, that's negative reinforcement. Positive reinforcement supports a person's good behavior. It gets him to do more of what we like, such as coming to work on time or catching difficult passes for long-yardage touchdowns.

There's a good reason for this. Harvard psychologist B. F. Skinner, the father of behavior modification, believes you can work only with what you can see, feel and touch—not with abstract theoretical constructs. He should have been a quarterback. Like him, I find the methods that work and the results you can see are what win games.

That's why, if you praise people for doing something, they are likely to do it again. For your reinforcement to work, it has to be *specific, sincere, immediate, personal, individual* and *proportional* to the behavior you are trying to reinforce.

I thought I did this all the time on the playing field. I thought I knew how to reinforce my offensive players properly. If Homer Jones ran a great pattern and caught one of my passes for good yardage, I might utter some masterful phrase such as "Good catch, Homer." Sometime later, I learned the right way to do it. When Homer got back into the huddle, I would say, "Homer, you're responsible for the yardage we got on that play because you ran a great pattern."

Homer already knew he'd run a great pattern, but he was now surprised and gratified to hear that *I knew it, too!* I individualized the reinforcement—it was strictly to Homer, not to the whole offensive team. It was personal, coming directly from me. I was sincere. I was immediate—I told him right after the play, not at the end of the game or during the Monday films or sometime the next year. And I was specific—it was the *pattern*, not just the general act of catching a pass, that I reinforced. It was also proportional—I didn't mumble as if it were no big deal and didn't jump up and down as if we had just won the Super Bowl. Anything disproportionate will not be taken seriously.

Here's the key: positive reinforcement is generally more effective than punishment. In fact, under ideal circumstances you would entirely ignore what a person is doing wrong and concentrate only on what he is doing right. Sometimes that person is so taken aback that his "right" behavior increases quickly and the "wrong" behavior is simply squeezed out without ever being attacked. Imagine if you *warmly* welcomed the chronically absent employee back to the workplace every time he was gone without even mentioning his absence. Concentrate on his *presence*, and ignore his *absence*. What you want is more *presence*, not a battle royal over his absence. Remember, as in sports, you're playing a results-oriented game. You're not trying to win wars of principle, but simply to change behavior.

Praise can come directly or in other forms: memos of commendation, presentation of the results of someone's good work at a meeting, a notice or picture on the bulletin board (such as the "Employee of the Month" notice used by some companies), positive comments on the graph charts and even approaching an employee for his advice or opinion. Invite the employee to join you in a coffee break; send birthday or anniversary cards to his home; inquire about the welfare of his family.

The single greatest lesson I've learned is that *people want to be cared about*. People need attention, they need to know how they are doing, and not only the doffers and spinners working on the production line. Middle managers, top managers, even the chief executive officers and chairmen of the board need reminding of their beauty spots.

FACT: *People don't want praise so much as attention*—you gotta care!

6.

MYTH: *Managers Should Manage Themselves*

The guy who gets the least feedback in any company is not the mailboy—it's the chief executive officer. Does he need the least? (Does buy low mean sell high?) Pity the poor CEO! There he sits in the executive suite trying to figure out ways to sincerely reinforce dozens or hundreds of people who work under him. But who reinforces the boss? In football, the joke is that the coach gets constant feedback, most of it in the form of eleven guys running around the field with his paycheck.

Believe it or not, the president of one of America's best-known financial services institutions once told me, "Fran, I've been here for two years now, and I still don't know how I'm doing. Nobody ever tells me."

When your boss does something that helps your business, he needs stroking just as much as the lowliest floor-sweeper in the company. When he does something for you, don't take him for granted. A lot of people think, "Well, that's his job." But, just like you, he needs to hear it when he is doing something right. The problem, of course, is that we are all in awe of our bosses. We think that because the boss has power and money, he must have the whole world by the tail. Because he's my boss, he doesn't need reinforcement.

Nothing could be further from the truth. Roberto Goizueta, chairman of the giant Coca-Cola Company, once described the dilemma of the CEO in America: "The way he is viewed...is a curse.... The press, employees, shareholders and the public all treat him—perhaps subconsciously—as a god. But if he starts behaving like one, they resent it."

Because we put the mighty CEO on such an out-of-reach pedestal, the boss often doesn't get the feedback and reinforcement he needs from his own subordinates. Like you, he needs a scoreboard on which to measure his performance.

One of the most common refrains I have heard from top executives over the years is, "I don't really know how well I am doing." Of course the boss has the bottom line and the profit-and-loss sheet to look at, but he also needs to know on a more intimate basis how well he is doing with immediate employees—with you.

Even NFL quarterbacks need reinforcement. Once I threw a key block in a game the Vikings won against the St. Louis Cardinals. During the Monday films I kept waiting for the coach to point out my contribution to that critical play. He praised the linemen and the runners and the water boy and the pom-pom girls, it seemed, but he never mentioned me and my key block.

I went to him after the team meeting and said, "Coach, why didn't you say anything about my block?"

"Fran," he said, "you always give a hundred and fifty percent. You're out there gung-ho all the time. So I just didn't feel that I needed to praise you for it."

"If you ever want me to do it again, you did," I said.

You can't always assume that even your most enthusiastic players are feeling good about themselves. They may give 150 percent, but they need to hear it if you're pleased. And thinking good thoughts about that member of your team is not enough—nobody can read your mind!

It may even inspire the players to praise the boss.

FACT: *Don't be afraid of the boss—he needs you too.*

7.

MYTH: *Macho Makes the Man a Manager*

Like most businessmen, you think you should be able to solve your problems all by yourself. You're not allowed any weaknesses or failings. You should maintain an all-knowing facade and fear doing anything that might make you appear less than perfect before your troops. Given all this, you must monopolize power for yourself.

Have I just written your unofficial job description? I wish I hadn't. This attitude has led to a dictatorial mentality among some managers. Instead of treating everyone they meet as if he were a CEO, they treat people like raw recruits in boot camp. Managers like this think they are Gen. George S. Patton roaring across the face of Europe. Rather than opening communications, this merely makes people duck and avoid the boss. It's like what Detroit Lions coach Monte Clark once said of hard-driving, all-pro fullback Larry Csonka: "When he goes on a safari, the lions roll up their windows."

Why does this approach appeal to so many managers? Perhaps they think that in football, the best leaders are the toughest ones—the yellers and the screamers. But great coaches such as Tom Landry and Bud Grant got the most out of their players with different tactics, namely, reserve and respect. Landry feels that players need emotion to perform optimally. But not coaches, for whom yelling is wasted energy. Another winning coach, USC's John McKay, once asked, "Does a team have to be emotional to win? After all, nobody is more emotional than my wife, Corky, and she can't play football worth a damn."

Any quarterback who thinks he can order his teammates around like cattle and still get maximum cooperation and effort out of them is in for a long, hard season. No ball player or manager can work well with his troops if he thinks and acts as though he alone has all the answers. On the contrary, when you treat the people you work with as though they were family, you can increase their sense of involvement in productivity and their respect for you as a leader. At Delta Airlines, a very successful company noted for its familylike feeling, even new hirings are made with this sensitivity in mind. Says chairman David Garrett: "One of the things we look for is that ability to *care* for others."

People assume that in football, intimidation is as integral to the game as air in the ball. But in fact, the opposite tactic often works better. I remember an encounter with lineman Mean Joe Greene when he was just a young, up-and-coming tough guy for the Pittsburgh Steelers.

The first time I played against Joe, he got thrown out of the game for hitting me full-blast after I had run out-of-bounds. I thought to myself, "It is possible to get killed by this man. I'd better be nice to him."

In our next game against the Steelers, Joe sacked me with a shot that made my head vibrate. As I got up, I said, "Nice tackle, Joe." A while later he got me again with another bell ringer. I said, "Good one, Joe. Man, I've been hearing a lot of good things about you." Third tackle— boom! But I still didn't give up. I said, "You know, Joe, you're really the soul of this team."

Joe got up and looked around at the capacity crowd in the stadium and said to me, "Hey, Fran, you really know how to pack 'em in, don't you?"

My last compliment to Joe had finally clicked. He was a little gentler with me from then on. Where would a mean macho approach have gotten me in that situation against Mean Joe? Unlike business, pro football can be like nuclear warfare: no winners, only survivors. If you think that *tough guys win;* that the louder you yell, the harder (and better) everyone will work; that if you chew people out and get on their asses a lot, that makes you a leader—you're wrong. It's like spanking a child to get a quick reaction even though the long-term response to corporal punishment may not be the one you want.

I remember a depressing moment on one of my teams. During a game, I got sacked just when a receiver had gotten open in the end zone for what could well have been the winning touchdown. I was hit before I could throw the pass because one of our linemen, an all-pro guard, missed his block.

On Monday morning when we were watching the films, the offensive line coach turned off the projector and chewed out the guard in front of all his teammates. He accused him of losing the game for us because he "didn't care enough." He claimed the defensive player was a harder worker with more character, and even made some insulting comments about our player's mother and father.

Now, what did the coach accomplish? Did he do anything to help that guard avoid missing a block in the next game? No. All the coach did was make *himself* feel good by showing everybody what a tough guy he was. In the process, he destroyed the player's confidence and broke his self-respect before his peers. And, in fact, that guard never played really well after that.

What other approach could that coach have taken? He could have said, "Okay, right guard, you missed that block. You missed it because your technique was bad, your stance was too narrow, you moved off balance and he came through you. So you're going to work on widening your base this week so that won't happen again."

The guard would have been thinking, "Thank you, coach. Now you've given me a way to improve myself."

What the Tough Guy does not understand is that all-too-rare art of correcting people without destroying human dignity. He does not know how to be a leader without being a bully. The Tough Guy thinks chewing people out is a sign of strength—when it is actually a signal of weakness.

With the Tough Guy, people will merely keep the lowest possible profile and try to step out of his way, rather than raise performance. Because they become preoccupied with avoiding the wrath of this leader-by-oppression, they cannot concentrate on their own performance. Fresh thoughts and new ideas are immediately suppressed for fear of a chewing-out by the boss if he does not like the proposal. No one takes an initiative. The Tough Guy syndrome simply breeds sycophants and yesmen.

I often disarm the tough guys I have come to deal with by opening my spiel with questions. Before long, they are completely wrapped up in a conversation with me, pouring out every detail of their desires and ideas, feeling completely involved with me as a partner—not as a boss or sales adversary. Asking questions gives you a chance to find out what it is that really turns that person on and is likely to get his commitment to you—as employee or customer. But when you start giving more answers than questions, you begin to fall into the trap of the expert.

Some managers think that being a success with people is a natural skill. Each of us likes to say, "I'm a 'people person,'" because most of us like other people and feel popular with our peers. But business is a great deal more than simply being nice to people. Cheerleaders are great on the sidelines of a football field, but cheerleaders don't call the plays or carry the ball. Whoever thinks he can manage through cheerleading alone is just as misguided as the macho man.

The Gladhander is the fellow who has read Norman Vincent Peale's *The Power of Positive Thinking* and believes he can succeed largely by smiling at everyone and telling them what great jobs they are doing. "Hey, you're doing a great job," he'll say to anyone who comes near the water cooler or the men's room. And people know the Gladhander *does not know* whether they are working well or badly, hard or easy, carefully or carelessly. *Insincere praise*—reinforcement based not on specific data but on obvious ignorance—*is more demoralizing than no praise at all!* The Gladhander undermines the respect of people by telling them things they don't believe.

Toughness in business means mental concentration and willingness to pay true attention to performance and to correct it through measurement and reinforcement. We all crave attention, right? *True attention* is not the kind of false, fleeting flattery the Gladhander gives; it is, rather, the time and effort it takes to measure a person's performance. It is the most impressive way to show that *you care*. A person would rather be told with accuracy and sincerity what he is doing wrong than be told he was doing something good when he knows better.

FACT: *No good advice has ever been given at the top of one's lungs.*

8.

MYTH: *Winners Don't Make Mistakes*

One of the greatest myths is that a winner wins all the time. On the contrary, I say that if you're never failing, *you're already on the road to failure!*

One thing any serious athlete will tell you is that *it's okay to lose!* Not only is it okay, but it is necessary. If you're never losing, you're never *stretching.* And if you don't stretch beyond your limits, you won't improve. To win, you've got to lose. To succeed, you've got to fail.

There is not a coach alive who doesn't scream this at you time and again, and who doesn't plan his game anticipating mistakes, or injuries or even a loss. In sports, injuries are one of our greatest enemies. Yet even sports injuries can heal to a strength greater than before the mishap.

Remember pitcher Tommy John? He recovered from a ruptured ligament and surgery in his pitching elbow with an even better arm than before he was hurt. Sportswriters started calling it "the bionic arm." "I never, never thought I was done," he says, and he wasn't. These remarkable recoveries happen because a player exercises the injured muscle or joint and concentrates his energy on healing it. And he never takes it for granted again.

Your mind and sense of business play are instruments just the same as Joe Theisman's arm or John Riggins's legs. You've got to get them skinned and bloodied and then stretch them again to find out how far you can go.

People like to quote Vince Lombardi's "Winning isn't everything, it's the only thing." But *Lombardi never said that*. Vanderbilt University coach Red Sanders did. Lombardi actually said something different: "Winning is not everything—but making the effort to win is."

Yet old Vince said something else that I agree with completely: "If you can't accept losing, you can't win." Lombardi understood a critical truth: that losing makes the winner. To become a winner and stay on top, you have to take risks and test yourself. Any time you try to reach beyond yourself, you will lose, a certain amount of the time. But that is how you become the better player—a winner.

I don't mean that you should be a good loser. As some smart businessman once said, "A good loser is a loser." What's important about how you play the game lies in what you learn from it. Let me give you an example.

I used to be pretty good at tennis, which was my recreational sport away from football. In fact, I could beat everybody in my playing bracket. Soon, though, I began to get bored with the game, until one day I realized I had to move up and take on better competition. To do that, *I had to start losing!* It was a frustrating, challenging and yet *fulfilling* experience. I stretched, I lost (several times) and—finally—I won. I went from being a B-plus player to a solid A.

Now I'm a ripe old retired quarterback and my sport is golf. I play about an eight handicap and am fighting for a six. Recently, I began to play some of the worst golf in my life. I wanted to throw my irons into the lake and push my putter all the way down into the cup. But I knew that something good was going to come of it: I was pushing for a better game, I was stretching, I was losing. And sure enough, several weeks later I was playing some of the best golf of my life—the low seventies on some days. Now I'm trying to hold on to that eight handicap.

It's okay to lose because *out of adversity come some of our greatest triumphs.* Consider Harry Gray, the chairman of United Technologies Corporation. Gray was born to a poor farming family in Milledgeville Crossroads, Georgia. When he was 6, his mother died; shortly thereafter his father left the family and he was almost abandoned and placed in an orphanage when his older sister, living in Chicago, decided to raise him. Out of this impoverished background, Gray worked his way through college and served in World War II under General Patton and now he's one of America's leading executives. He took a stagnating $2 billion company and remade it within a decade into a $14 billion one. Asked about his achievements, Harry admitted that one of the driving forces behind his success was, "I disliked being poor."

Almost all the great business successes of our time have had a low point in their past. James D. Robinson III, the whiz-kid chairman of American Express, bounced back from a much-criticized acquisition attempt a few years ago. He has since reshaped his company into a thriving combination of financial services. Could Jimmy have gone on not just to succeed, but to shine in such a big way if he hadn't learned so much from his earlier loss? I don't think so.

Yet many people are defeated by defeat. This is a natural reaction to adversity. If you lose, you forget that the game goes on tomorrow, the score rolls back to an even zero-zero, and you have another chance. Instead you think something is fundamentally wrong with you or your approach. Even an upbeat person like me had that problem once in a while. In football, you don't get to play that game again until next year.

Yet every time I began to feel like a loser, I

remembered the words of Bobby Layne, legendary quarterback of the Detroit Lions: "I never lost a game, I just ran out of time." Sure enough, you never completely lose a game, because there's always something a loss teaches you to do better.

Layne's comment is particularly appropriate in business, where you always have another chance tomorrow because there is no final gun. Think of your own times of adversity: facing down an angry board of directors, dealing with public ridicule or sustaining a business failure so terrible that you didn't want to go to work in the morning. Instead of letting these times defeat you, think of these as moments of greatest opportunity, the chance for the winner in you to truly show itself.

General Patton was right when he said, "The test of success is not what you do when you are on top. Success is how high you bounce when you hit bottom."

But there's something more important here: not just surviving mistakes—but facing up to the possibility of mistakes. Stretching means taking risks. Whenever you take risks, sometimes you fail. The tiger hiding in the bushes is more intimidating than the one you see in rifle-range. Overcoming the fear of mistakes is what risk-taking is all about.

Risk-taking is the opposite of gambling. Gambling is betting on luck; risk-taking is using your head. I make the distinction this way: When you look at a business deal from every point of view, figure out the maximum downside risk, determine that you can live with the worst possible scenario if it doesn't work out—then you can take that risk.

J. Peter Grace, chairman of W. R. Grace and Co., is a classic risk-taker. When he saw that his company's traditional South American shipping and mining operations were soon to be doomed by changing political and market conditions after World War II, he shocked the investment world by shifting W. R. Grace into wholly new and untried fields, such as specialty chemicals, one of the new growth industries. "When I went into the chemical business, I was criticized by Wall Street," he says. "They said, 'What's a steamboat outfit doing building petrochemical plants?' They were all laughing up their sleeve. But if we hadn't done that, we wouldn't be in business today."

Today W. R. Grace is not in a single one of the businesses it conducted back in 1945 when Peter took over. It has gone from fruit imports, copper mining and a large fleet of cargo ships into restaurant chains, sporting goods and high-tech chemical plants—all because Peter Grace was willing and bold enough to be a risk-taker. He says, "My basic philosophy is that you have to be big to take risks, and you have to take risks to grow."

I know. I've been at the bottom, sometimes with a ton of human flesh on top of me. But the time I really felt pressured the most was during all those winning years with the Minnesota Vikings in the 1970s. Why then? Because the more you win, the greater the pressure to continue winning. If you're not winning, nobody expects you to win, so you can go into a football game with the attitude "What have we got to lose?"

But we were winning so much at Minnesota during the 1970s that the pressure got to me. Finally I decided the way to deal with it was to get psyched by saying to myself, "So what if we lose? It's not a big deal. I don't care. I'm just going to go out there and play my football game. If they beat us a hundred to zip, more power to them. But I won't let them win a hundred to nothing because I'm so scared of losing that I just warm my backside and don't take risks—even to the point of making a mistake. After all these years in the game, I still haven't figured how to get into the end zone when I'm on my rear end."

I was practically saying these things *out loud* to myself in the locker room before the games. They helped me reach a point where I could play with the fear of losing. The result: we had another winning season.

Business executives often feel the same kind of pressure that I was under. The farther you rise on the corporate ladder, the more you have that you don't want to give up. Winning breeds caution; paranoia rises with corporate status. You achieve position, social standing, power, money, club memberships and a nice standard of living. So, all of a sudden, you start making conservative, low-risk choices. You become an ordinary businessman masquerading in an extraordinary title. You don't want to offend or lose a client. You don't want to rub any associates or superiors the wrong way. You conform. *You quit taking risks.* That's when you start getting left behind. Sooner or later, you get left out of the lineup.

I contend that risk-taking is what made this country great. The people who came over to settle America—where did they come from? They came from nothing. They were running away from a class system where all they knew was defeat, to find a new chance in a new land. They were entrepreneurial spirits. They did crazy things like invent electricity and the light bulb. They took the horse and buggy and came up with mass-produced cars even before we had highways. Those crazy Wright brothers gave up bicycles and started flying a strange machine around the beaches of North Carolina.

Then you know what happened? American business got big and powerful and cautious. We started thinking like accountants who are bossed by lawyers who warn, "We've got to be safe from all these laws and make sure we handle things just right." Would one of these guys hire a risk-taker like Henry Ford today? Would the Ford Motor Company? They'd be afraid of his daring spirit and the possibility he would make mistakes. One CEO I know of actually signed up for flying lessons because his business was going so well that he was worried he'd lose his risk-taking edge. Fortunately, there are still some entrepreneurial risk-takers in American business. Lew Lehr, the chairman of 3M, also recognized the value of taking risks, stretching and failing when he said: "Flops are valuable in certain ways. Someone said, 'You can learn from success, but you have to work at it; it's a lot easier to learn from failure.'"

That is so true. One of the tests of a true winner is the player who *wins and stretches*, not the one who stretches only when he has begun losing. Roger Milliken, chairman of the giant Milliken & Co. textile chain based in South Carolina, is a classic example of the winner who stretches. Even when leading his industry, Roger is constantly on the lookout for ways to change, improve or diversify his company. He does not sit back on his old successes and replay last year's victories in his head. Roger is always searching.

An example of a team that was winning but did not stretch is the American automobile industry. It stuck to its "proven" success formula for much too long. While Detroit was wedded to the time-honored idea of the big American gas guzzler, the Japanese and Europeans were quietly building themselves a whopping share of the American car market with a new kind of transportation: small, efficient, loaded with little luxuries. Satisfied that they alone understood and controlled the tastes of the American car buyer, our manufacturers ceased searching and soon began to lose.

Fortunately, Detroit has awakened and is changing today—with change itself. "We're not resisting change," says General Motors chairman Roger Smith, "we're embracing it."

Even in sports, many people make the mistake of stretching only when they're down. The classic case is the San Francisco Giants, who stretched and won under coach Bill Walsh and became the Cinderella victors of the 1982 Super Bowl. The following year, they were in the cellar and did not even make the play-offs. They had not learned the fundamental rule that you must *stretch even when you're ahead*; it cost them dearly even while they were the defending champions.

FACT: *The good news: It's okay to lose.*

9.

MYTH: *A Winner Never Quits*

You have no doubt heard the old bromide "Quitters never win and winners never quit." While I am a great believer in dogged, unrelenting tenacity, I don't believe wholeheartedly in this little slogan. It is just another piece of our over-inflated sense of macho in business and in sports. The truth is, we are all quitters. The sooner we realize it, the better. Then we can get on with the business of overcoming it.

Some wise man once said that it's easier to start a love affair than to end one. Sometimes you have to quit—and sometimes it's the hardest but most important thing to do.

Let me tell you about the time I quit. It was in my next-to-last year in football, the 1977–78

season. The Vikings had lost their third Super
Bowl with me as quarterback the season before.
Never mind that it was me at the helm during all
those winning games that got us into the Super
Bowl in the first place; the Minnesota fans had
decided Tarkenton was the reason they still
didn't have that football-on-a-pedestal Super Bowl
trophy in the local clubhouse. And they decided
that Tarkenton had to go. People used to come
up to me on the street and in restaurants to tell
me so. I could not put a bite of steak in my
mouth without somebody who thought he knew
more football than I did coming up to criticize
and coach me so that we would never lose
another Super Bowl. It reached the point that I
just stopped going out in public.

Our third game of that season was against
the Tampa Bay Buccaneers. Tampa Bay had
come into the league the year before as an
expansion team and had lost every game. Now
they were in Minnesota playing the mighty
Vikings—and we were losing in the fourth quarter! Our great team had gotten a little bit older
and we were simply not as good anymore. Jim
Marshall and the great front four of our defense
had their finest days behind them. We were
struggling. In the fourth quarter, I think all
47,000 people in our stadium stood up and booed
me.

I'll never forget that day. I had suffered
some mighty booing in Yankee Stadium during
my final season with the New York Giants in

1971. But nothing hurt me so much as the sound of those Vikings fans I had loved so much calling for my head on a platter during this game. Worse, they were shouting for Bud Grant to put in Tommy Kramer, the backup quarterback. "We want Kramer! We want Kramer!" echoed back and forth across that old erector set of a stadium in Bloomington, Minnesota. That we lost the game did not help any, either.

I came off the field that day more depressed than I had ever been. I was angry with myself and angry with the fans. I was calling them no-good assholes and worse. I let them get under my skin. *I let them control me!*

The shouts for Kramer kept echoing through my head all Sunday night, so much that I couldn't even sleep. The next morning I walked into Bud Grant's office and said, "I'm going to Atlanta and I'm not coming back." I was quitting.

He said, "You think about it and I'll call you at three o'clock tomorrow afternoon."

Well, the next day Bud called me in Atlanta at three o'clock. I said, "I've thought about it and I'm still quitting. I don't have to put up with the crap anymore. I've given this organization all I've got, and what do the people give me in return—boos and yelling for Kramer. I'm not going to play anymore."

Bud just said, "Well, Fran, I wish I had some magic word to tell you that would make you come back and play. But I don't. I just hope you understand that if you don't come back, we have no chance to make the play-offs this year."

Well, that really hit me! I thought to myself, "You selfish son of a bitch. Here you have forty-four teammates out there. Old Tingelhoff and Marshall are up there busting their backsides. They're old and tired and they're still trying. And just because you got booed, you're going to run off and throw their chances to the wolves."

I just hung up and packed my bags. Got the next plane back to Minneapolis. Never said a word to anyone, just showed up for Wednesday practice. Most people never knew I was gone, never knew I had quit.

Everybody quits. We've all got some quit in us. It is a normal human reaction. Luckily for me, I had a coach who was sensitive enough to find the trigger point that brought me back.

The trick, it seems to me, is not to say, "Winners never quit." On the contrary, winners are the people who recognize the desire every one of us has to quit when faced with adversity and who develop ways of dealing with it. I have never met an athlete or a competitor of any kind whose first impulse isn't to quit when things are not going well. There were times in the middle of a game, when I couldn't seem to complete any of the important passes, when I just said to myself, "I just can't get this job done, it ain't worth it, I want to quit." It's part of everyday life.

In business, salesmen go through this all the

time. They get so many doors slammed in their faces and have a sales slump. One prospect shouts at him over the phone: "Don't call me again! I'm tired of hearing from you!" The salesman begins to drag. He makes fewer sales calls. He walks more slowly. He loses his mental toughness. His business begins to slide. *He has let the outside pressures get to him.*

This is the same as letting the booing fans in the stadium shape my attitude toward the game: I quit. This is what happens to the salesman in his slump. That's the time to remember those good weeks and months that have gone before. Your inner knowledge of yourself is the most important source of power you have. You have to control your attitude, not let others do it for you.

I think there is a great lesson for managers here in the way Coach Grant handled me. A lot of coaches might have gotten angry and called me a no-good bastard and said they were glad I was gone. That would have sealed it: if Bud had said something like that to me, I never would have come back. But because he had sensitive understanding and common sense, Bud not only got me back, he got me playing better football for the rest of the season. We *did* make the play-offs that year!

Bud's great compassionate management style wasn't gushy; it was sincere and specific—totally businesslike. He didn't tell me I had a bad attitude, he merely showed me what the results of my quitting might be. (Remember how we pointed out earlier that scorekeeping means distinguishing between behaviors and the *results* of those behaviors.)

Bud always reminded me of one of America's other great managers: Robert W. Woodruff, the legendary chairman emeritus of the Coca-Cola Company. I worked there briefly as a junior executive in their management-training program during the off-seasons of 1966–67. I learned a lot at Coca-Cola. One lesson I learned there was that quitting could give you fresh perspective on yourself, could even make you feel like a self-starter, a winner. Mr. Woodruff knew this, too. Once he called in the entire sales force and told them in no pretty terms that the sales department was being abolished and that they were jobless. If they felt like quitters and acted like quitters, he'd force them to quit—as simple as that. But Mr. Woodruff told them to report the next morning for their final instructions.

The former salesmen retired uneasily to their hotels. When they reassembled the next day, Woodruff announced that the company was forming a service department and would welcome their applications for jobs in it. The message Woodruff delivered was that their job was not just *selling* Coca-Cola, but *servicing* their customers' needs. He got the reps to surpass their performance by showing them that if they gave less than 100 percent, they were quitters. And feeling less than 100 percent committed made them feel less than the best—so why not recognize that and start again? They did, and turned Coca-Cola into the world's best selling product. Woodruff's successors have calculated that if all the Coca-Cola ever consumed by the human race were poured over Niagara Falls, "the Falls would flow at their normal rate for eight hours and fifty-seven minutes." Not bad for a bunch of quitters.

FACT: *Quitting is not the opposite of winning—it's part of winning.*

10.

MYTH: *For Big Successes, Risk the Big Play*

Let me make one thing clear right now: I don't believe in the *big play*. In fact, with very few exceptions I don't think there is any such thing as a planned big play.

Let's start with football. You hear the term "big play" all the time on television. "St. Louis needs a big play right here," intones my buddy Howard Cosell from time to time. What Howard means, of course, is that the Cardinals are in some kind of hole with the clock grinding down, and only the breakaway run or long bomb pass over everybody's head will save the game for them.

This is desperation football. This is the only situation in which "big play" truly applies. By definition, if you're playing desperation football, you're in trouble. It means that your team didn't do something else right earlier in the game. Being forced to go for the big play is almost the definition of failure. It is the last grasping for straws that will overcome all your previous deficiencies.

If winning by big plays is a team's conscious strategy, it is doomed to a losing season. The game is sixty minutes long, so each team has time to institute a sound game plan, carry out long drives based on reasonable gains and win with solid football, not big plays. Big plays cannot be planned or forced; they just happen.

The big play is the football equivalent of the businessman who gambles the mortgage on the single venture—one product line, one high-stakes real estate deal, a single technological innovation—to catapult his company into high profitability. It may work occasionally, but as a rule this is the route to business failure. No less a business giant than shipping magnate D. K. Ludwig learned this lesson to his sorrow when he overreached on the development of huge tracts of the Brazilian jungle, a venture which he finally had to abandon.

A perfect example of a company that develops a sound game plan and tries to make reasonable gains with a solid business repertoire is The 3M Company of Minneapolis. Rather than throw all its eggs into the single basket of a big play, this multifarious Minnesota manufacturer keeps a highly varied product line on the market and is constantly renewing it with innovative products. This strategy has been called "nichemanship." It is based on the principle that at least 25 percent of the company's revenues should at all times be derived from new products. With a new product defined as one less than five years old, this stimulates a constant, ongoing search in the marketing and research divisions for new ways to serve the consumer. This is a company that *stretches* rather than looks for salvation in the long ball.

I learned early, the hard way, that the big play is not only an unreliable approach to football but that it can have a negative effect on the rest of your game. In my second game as a rookie quarterback for the Minnesota Vikings, we were playing Dallas, themselves a lowly expansion team only the year before. I was still riding high from our opening-game upset victory over the Chicago Bears the week before, smug in the certainty of my invincibility in the National Football League. And sure enough, on our first series of downs, I reached back and threw a long "bomb" for a 70-yard touchdown.

I thought, "Heck. This is easy. I'll just do things like that all day."

We never scored again that day, and the Cowboys beat us like a drum, 21–7.

The big plays that do occur in football are, often as not, accidental. There is, I suppose, such a thing as a true big play, but even they emerge naturally from a series of other small things you have done right. Once, at fourth and 1 on the other team's 45-yard line, I called a quarterback sneak—and ran for a touchdown! That play is designed to gain exactly 1 yard—but it accidentally became a big play.

On the blackboard and in the playbook, every play is designed to be the big play. Every offensive play shows the ball carrier continuing like a straight arrow down the field. We have X's and O's; we have blocking symbols and dotted lines; but we have no symbol in the offensive playbooks for a *tackle!* We score every time!

Thank God, I learned early not to live by the big play alone. If you look back at my career statistics, you'll see that my longevity and record-setting in the game were based not on the spectacular big plays, but on steady execution of the proven ground-gainers: short passes and consistent running plays. My old nemesis, the late Norm Van Brocklin, recognized early that I didn't have the arm for the 30-yard pass toward the sidelines (an "out ball"), and one day he told me so. "Tarkenton," he said, "you can't get ten pounds of manure into a one-pound bag." After that, I concentrated on the short balls across the middle and on quick-outs to the flats.

But not all quarterbacks are fortunate enough to learn this important lesson. Even one of my own teammates seemed to suffer from a love affair with the big play. Bobby Lee, like all the backup quarterbacks I played with for eighteen years, had a stronger arm and better physical gifts than I. He was 6 feet, 2 inches tall and 200 pounds. His frozen-rope passes made mine look like loose clothesline. But Bobby Lee never became a permanent starting quarterback who could lead a team to victory. Why? Because, with all his strength, he had fallen in love with the big play: the long ball that wins the game in glory and style. As a result, Bobby remained a journeyman quarterback all his career.

The same thing happens in business all the time. A company has a problem. It looks for a cure-all solution, a quick panacea that will drive the demons away overnight and bring success in the front door like a Heisman Trophy. As often as not, the result is early insolvency.

All of us have heard stories of the man who invented the better mousetrap and got rich quick. America is in love with its Horatio Alger legend. Even today, we hear these stories in the burgeoning computer field. I believe in risk-taking entrepreneurship, but these are the rare dream tales—the wonder boys who are in the right place at the right time. If football taught me anything about business, it is that *you win the game one play at a time.*

Your chances of success in business by the magic method are about as great as those of the ghetto kids who all think they are Magic Johnson or Tony Dorsett. Tennis champion Arthur Ashe constantly reminds them that there are only a few hundred full-time professional athletes making big money in America in any given year, and that banking on sports to pull them into the mainstream is like dealing with play money. He tells them to hone their skills in school for a successful life in other fields. Likewise, the good businessman is constantly learning from others the details and solid plays that will make his company go. The big play is strictly fool's gold.

Maybe it was my lack of outstanding physical prowess that helped me so much in the game. I learned early that I could not live by my arm, my speed or my strength. I had to learn to live by my wits. I scrambled.

Scrambling is the opposite of the big play. It is like the street kid trying to figure out how to start a lemonade stand when he hears about a summertime parade five minutes after it has started. It is a readiness to adapt and turn what appears to be a losing situation to your advantage. Scrambling, truth to tell, is what most of us do all the time in our lives. Being a scrambler is a sure teacher that you cannot live by the big play.

Norm Van Brocklin taught me a corollary lesson. Whenever he saw me trying to make too much out of a play, he said, "You'll never go broke taking a profit."

Van Brocklin was talking the language of the stock market on the football field. He was trying to teach me a simple lesson: don't go for 15 risky yards when you can get 5 sure ones. It is a principle of the marketplace that you will never fail if you take your gains modestly but consistently. The people who go broke and jump out of skyscraper windows are the ones who gambled on the big play and got burned—badly.

Big plays are just that—gambling. Gambling is for Las Vegas. Risk-taking is for business. The difference between the two is that the risk-taker knows both his downsides and his upsides. The gambler is praying for help from Lady Luck.

When in doubt, remember that in football an 80-yard drive is better than an 80-yard "bomb." The bomb—the long pass that scores a touchdown—can be dismissed by the other team as a lucky, one-time fluke, which it probably is. The sustained drive that systematically pushes the other team back over its own goal line shows them that you play sound, unbeatable football, and is far more demoralizing to your opposition.

The smart leader sets visible, reasonably attainable goals for his sports or business team and lets the greater victory take care of itself. Jimmy Robinson at American Express is known for outlining his company's long-term strategy but getting his people to focus on short-term targets. With some 45,000 products on the market, 3M is the classic example of a team that beats the world with an endless string of small, good plays—remember Scotch Tape!—rather than banking heavily on a single money cow. "We're a nickels-and-dimes company," laughs international operations president James A. Thwaits.

"We don't have many big-ticket items." And yet 3M is a $6 billion company!

Winning the big games in business or sports with a series of steady, small victories is a surer route to success than gambling your mortgage on the big play. He who lives by the big play will die by it.

FACT: *Beware the big play: The 80-yard drive is better than the 80-yard pass.*

11.

MYTH: *Superstars Can Carry the Team*

One of the greatest myths in sports is that superstars can win alone. In such individual sports as golf and tennis, this may be true—yet even Tom Watson and John McEnroe have their coaches, trainers and even their caddies.

But business is not an individual game. *Business is a team sport.* Every CEO, no matter how brilliant, is utterly dependent on the commitment and teamwork of his players to win his games. No football player ever became a superstar without ten other guys on the field to make him one. Even during the years when I was regarded as one of the star quarterbacks of the National Football League, I was dependent on my teammates in far more ways than most fans imagine.

I learned early that the most important things a quarterback does are not the physical ones of passing and ball-handling. On the contrary, what made me a star was teamwork. I discovered that the critical factor in generating teamwork is to *get everyone involved*. All of us together, in business and in sports, are smarter than any one of us alone.

Involvement is not an automatic thing. It is easy enough for a quarterback or running back to get excited every time he handles the ball, but how do you get the involvement of the lineman who can't point to his pass completions or rushing yardage at the end of the game? How does an offensive guard or tackle know what his contribution is to the final score? How can you involve your lineman, in the factory or on the field, in winning on a minute-by-minute basis? After all, the points go up throughout the game, not simply at the end of play.

I wondered about these things when I returned to the Minnesota Vikings in 1972. I wanted ways of making the game more manageable. Otherwise, it becomes bigger than you can handle. As University of North Carolina basketball coach Dean Smith used to joke, "If you make every game a life-or-death situation, you're going to have problems. For one thing, you'll be dead a lot." So I found the ways.

Maybe more than anything else, I concentrated on the small plays and made sure they were executed correctly. I told Homer Jones why he had done a good job on a certain pass play. If my right guard, Darrell Dess, was going nose-to-nose with mean Bob Lilly, I let Darrell know it every time I saw him keeping Lilly out of my face on a passing play. Just as a manager has no job, no product and nothing to manage without his staff, I had no chance of throwing a pass—no chance of even being a quarterback— without Darrell doing the job of protecting me from Lilly. After a critical play involving a rush by Lilly, I would go up to Dess and tell him specifically, "Darrell, that play worked because you kept Big Bob off my rear end. Thanks."

Whether we won or lost, Darrell helped win that minute for us. Realizing that would help him add another winning minute to the score.

But praising performance after the fact has its limitations, too. Sometimes you might have to wait a long time for just the right performance to reinforce. That's when *involvement* becomes important. It brings your players into the action before they have made the outstanding play. It sets them up to make that play.

It's one thing to involve your people in a quality circle where they set common goals and can watch one another's performance in attaining them—especially if most members of the group work at the same job. But every member of a football team has a different job on every play and has to come up with individual performance. The traditional structure of a football offense puts the coach and quarterback—the managers—in charge and expects everyone else to do his job on command. Vikings offensive coordinator Jerry Burns and I decided to change that a little bit.

The great unsung heroes of any football team are its offensive linemen. They are the hod carriers, the engine room crew, the dog shift of the team. On the Washington Redskins 1983 Super Bowl championship team, its celebrated front line was known as "the Hogs" because they were always "rooting around in the mud." These guys expected to get into those trenches and wage unrewarded warfare for sixty minutes every Sunday afternoon without complaint—and without much praise. But how do you give these "hogs" a sense of participation in the whole slugfest?

Burnsie and I began giving jobs to the linemen. Mick Tingelhoff, my center and one of my best friends for thirteen years, used to joke about "Fran making a fortune with his hands up my ass." The good news, Tingelhoff always added, was, "I liked it." Anyway, Tingelhoff had the job of setting the huddle. Nothing could begin toward the next play until Mick decided where to line us up behind the line of scrimmage. This is the center's traditional job and it gives him a sense of participation in running the offense.

Then we took Ron Yary, our right tackle, and made it his specific job to break the huddle. It was Yary's job to get us right up to the line of scrimmage on every play. Now Yary wasn't just another hunk of meat beating up on another hunk of meat every Sunday, but he was actually in charge of something. He was involved in running the offense.

We put right guard Ed White in charge of getting us properly aligned on the line of scrimmage. This had the obvious effect of helping to avoid offsides penalties and of making sure we lined up as a single wall, but it also got Ed involved in the production of every play. It gave him a responsibility. If the Monday films showed a ragged lineup, or that we got off the ball in an irregular fashion, Coach Burns would remind White that this was his job. That's accountability.

But there was more. I involved my offensive linemen in actually calling the plays. Though I had the reputation in the National Football League of being a good play-caller, the truth is that my teammates called 70 percent of the plays. Tactical decisions on the playing field or in the boardroom are normally the job of management, right? As quarterback, I had the right to call all the plays and expect every man on the team to keep his mouth shut and run whatever I decided. But instead, I got them involved in management. After all, each player knew what was going on at his position better than I did.

If I needed short yardage, I might turn to Yary and say, "Okay Ron, can we get it?" He might say, "The guy's playing me hard on the outside shoulder. I can get it for you on the inside." Snap, bam, 2 yards. Thank you, Mr. Yary.

I learned not to be the macho manager who thinks he has all the answers. I could have told Ahmad Rashad, my wide receiver, "Okay, Ahmad, run a twenty-yard out pattern and let's get a first down." Of course, Ahmad has been running out there all afternoon and he knows the defensive back is playing his outside and there is no way in the world he can run a 20-yard *out* pattern successfully. But *I* have told him to because *I* am the leader. I am the quarterback. I am the boss. "You go do it!"

Ahmad might be thinking, "Okay, you dumb ass. You're making me run this pattern. I'll go through the motions, but *I am going to be defeated.*"

How often does that happen in business because bosses are unwilling to involve their people in calling the plays? Or because co-workers won't share responsibility? Wouldn't it be a little bit smarter if I said, "Okay, Ahmad, what have you got?"

Ahmad might say, "I can run a twenty-yard curl-in." Now, this guy has better input than I do. I'm back here being chased around by these Bob Lillys and Too-Tall Joneses. Things get kind of confused back there. But Ahmad is downfield on every play—he *knows* what is going on. *He* can call that play better than I can—and he does. Boom, 20 yards, first down. Thanks, Mr. Rashad.

Letting Ahmad call those plays never guaranteed their success, of course. But at least I knew that on that play I had his involvement *to the hilt*. I knew he wasn't just doing what management told him to do. By involving him, I had gotten his commitment to the plan and I knew he was going to do the best job he could. I was simply doing what Jack Welch, chairman of General Electric, calls "breaking down the barriers of corporate protocol so that anyone with a good idea feels that he or she has the freedom to communicate it with anyone else." That's involvement—sharing the play-calling. Roger Smith, the chairman of General Motors, has had to learn the lessons of not involving the work force in corporate planning the hard way—by loss of market share to imported cars. Now he puts the situation quite bluntly: "Encouraging worker ideas and participation in decision-making is no longer just an option for American business—it's a necessity."

But back to football. You remember how we posted charts beside the spinning frames to give the doffers a scorecard? Well, we decided to do the same thing with our offense in Minnesota. We broke successful offensive football down into its component parts by examining the performance of the four top play-off teams in the League over the previous four years. Here are some of the specific areas we concentrated on:

We found that the winning teams had always averaged 4 *yards per carry* on the ground.

They had always gained at least *100 yards rushing* and *200 yards passing* per game. We figured out how often they had scored after getting *inside the 15-yard line* without turning over the football. We found that our chances of being scored against after *punting from inside our own 20-yard line* were much greater than if we punted from beyond our own 20-yard line. By working up a chart on each of these specifics of the winning game, we were able to concentrate on each small component of success, not simply on the overall goal of winning.

At first, some of the coaches didn't believe the chart would work. They said, "Hey, these are big grown men making seventy thousand a year. Why do they care about a Mickey Mouse chart on the wall? What are you going to give them for making each of these goals?"

My answer was, "Nothing. All we give them is feedback and reinforcement."

The chart became a great reinforcer. Every Monday morning, the offensive players went to this great chart on the locker room wall, saying, "How did we do?" We got a point for every box that was checked off. Out of twenty categories of winning, sometimes we had 18 points. Those were usually games that we had won. Sometimes we made only 4 or 5 of our checkpoints—and usually had lost those games (or the defense had won them for us).

Because my teammates were working for achievement of specific and attainable goals which they knew would lead to victory most of the time, they became intent on performing better. And so did I! Now I knew not to go for a 15-yard play on third and long inside our 20. I knew just to get the football out beyond the 20 so our punting team could give us some good defense and we might get the ball back without being scored against. All of us began concentrating on performance in ways that we could see, feel and measure. And we did it not for money, but for performance! What we wanted was success, and we knew it came in the so-called small plays—the plays that everybody on the team could measure.

There are great players but there aren't any superstars. Superstars you find somewhere out beyond the moon.

FACT: *It takes a team to make a superstar.*

12.

MYTH: *Listen to the Monday-Morning Quarterbacks*

Once when he was asked why Notre Dame had just lost a certain football game, the great Knute Rockne turned to his questioner and answered, "I won't know until my barber tells me on Monday."

The Monday-morning quarterback is truly the bane of the professional football player. I can't tell you how often fans have come up to me following a Vikings loss and told me how I should have played a game. And they included a few folks who looked as though they might have trouble running a short pattern to the fridge for their next can of beer. No matter— You pay your money, you get to complain. I just tried to stay out of public restaurants after any game where I'd thrown more than three interceptions and we had lost.

In football, you learn to ignore the second-guessers and get on with preparing for the next game the best way you know how. Any coach or quarterback who starts running his team according to the advice of his Monday-morning barber or the whims of the fans in the stands is on his way to a quick demise. Former NBA basketball coach Johnny Kerr put it this way: "If a coach starts listening to the fans, he winds up sitting next to them."

The same is obviously true for you and your business. There will always be a Monday-morning barber telling you when and how to change your strategy, your product, your location, your advertising or whatever. I recently counseled some friends of mine who run an extremely successful restaurant chain. I told them, "Everybody in the world thinks he has the secret of running a food and beverage business, for no better reason than that everybody eats and drinks. Every customer is going to give you some advice. Keep your ears open for the good ideas, but remember: *You are the experts.* When you violate your own best instincts because of outside pressures, you lose. Advice is cheap when the advisor does not have to suffer the consequences of his advice."

It was the same on the football field. I always looked for input from my offensive teammates for plays that would work in a particular situation. But in the end, I had to decide which play to call. I factored in the advice of my players, but then took responsibility and went with what my gut told me to do. I couldn't worry about the Monday-morning drones. They're experts at tracing the Johnstown flood to a leaky faucet in Altoona. After all, nobody is more knowledgeable about your situation than you. Don't let the second-guessers try to play your game for you. If they could, they'd be out there on the gridiron—not you.

Of course this does not always win you a lot of friends. My old teammate Ron Yary (now a Monday-morning quarterback himself) once criticized me for "not being a team player." He said that when I came to the Vikings, I concentrated more on the record books than on the welfare of the team. I called Ron up and asked him, "What is your definition of 'team'?" He said he just had a general feeling that I was playing more for myself than for the Vikings.

Then I asked him how many play-off checks he had picked up before I arrived back in Minnesota. "None," he said. How many after I left? "One." How many while I was quarterbacking the team? "Three."

I told Yary my fundamental belief: that it is the goal of any organization or team *to win*. The only purpose of a business is to turn a profit; the purpose of a football team is to beat other football teams. I may have made some decisions as quarterback that made some people mad and made other people experts at second-guessing me. But we won a lot of football games and took home bonus money, even though we never won the Super Bowl. Ron's response was: "I never thought of it that way." When you realize your chief goal is to win, that's when you become secure enough to stand up to your critics.

That's why I'd play on any team Harry Gray was on. Harry believes that if you "submit" to pressure from peers, you move down to their level. Speak up for your beliefs and you invite them up to your level. If you move with the crowd, you'll get no farther than the crowd. Indeed! I'm glad I never had to play *against* any of those Monday-morning quarterbacks. After all, they're tougher than anyone already on the team.

FACT: You, *not your barber, are the best Monday-morning quarterback.*

13.

MYTH: *"Talent Always Beats Experience"*

In business and in sports, trading on your experience *is* a talent. Experience helped me survive longer in the pros than most players. And my best lessons in experience were the result of studying my own mistakes. Far more important than the quarterbacks at the barber shop and in the restaurants is the one who can really do something about the problems: *you.* You are the only important quarterback in anything involving your own business. You are the one who has to learn to take stock on Monday morning and decide what must be done to win again, win more, win better.

The football quarterback does this nearly every week. Let me tell you, it can be a painful experience to sit in a room watching films on the day after a losing game with all the guys you work with every day. I've watched myself throw interceptions, fumble the football and call stupid plays. And I knew that fifty thousand other people had gone to bed the night before wondering how I could do those things. (So much for the great feeling of fellowship.) It's a brutal although sobering and instructive experience. Your belief in yourself nearly gets destroyed. You're like the golfer whose putting turns sour and he becomes convinced he can never sink another five-footer. But as soon as I could get over the embarrassment, I tried to turn Monday mornings into a learning experience. And the only way to rebuild my confidence before the next game was to *go back to basics.*

Whenever my confidence was shot, a return to the basics helped me establish a sense of perspective. For me, going back to basics might mean simplifying my game plan, improving my "reads" of the defense or practicing my footwork. Most often, it was in doing things I thought were instinctive that I'd slipped up on, like reading the defensive keys. Every quarterback is tempted after a while to think that he can "instinctively" pick out that fine seam in the defensive backfield and always throw the ball to the right man. But the truth is that this happens only with luck. If a quarterback tries to watch everybody, he sees nobody. Dark shirts and light shirts begin to blend, and then come the striped shirts of the officials. By now, the passer doesn't know where there's single coverage and double coverage.

There's nothing like seeing yourself in livid color on Monday morning throwing the ball to the fleet-footed guys on the other team to remind you of such basics as *reading your keys*. Most of the time, this means concentrating on the free safety or the middle linebacker, or both. Their moves will lead you to the weak spots in the defense. Reading keys is like flying on instruments in an airplane. You've got to trust what the radar is telling you. By forcing myself to concentrate once again on this long-taught fundamental of passing, I was able to break the successful play down into its components—and regain my confidence. Concentrate on the components of success, not on the abstract concept of winning!

You should use the same techniques in business. If you concentrate on the loss of sales, you're overlooking the fundamentals: prospecting, making calls, presentations and good closes. Are you asking for the buy? Or are you dodging your accountability by looking too much at the big picture and too little at the measurements of your performance? Most people only look at the annual report to see if the corporation won or lost that year. People ask, "Did we win or lose as a corporation?" You learn the results of your group effort, but how do you break it down for the guards and tackles? How does the line worker on the second shift at the Rouge plant in Detroit know whether *he* has won or lost, whether he has had any impact on General Motors' annual profits?

But this raises the question of how we get the data. Football is a unique profession in having an undeniable record in the form of films to study after every game. And the film never lies! But how do you get a "film" of your business?

This is where hands-on management and data-gathering become all-important. And this is where American business is still in the dark ages, running a single wing while the rest of society has already passed through the T formation and the I formation into the modern "shotgun" lineup. Many managers only get loose, outdated and excessive data about their operations. For all intents and purposes, they don't know what is going on in their companies. It's hard to be a good Monday-morning quarterback if you don't have a reliable "film."

There are two ways to change this. One is to set up detailed and continuous measures of performance (the P.R.I.C.E.). The other is through your own intimate contact with the people and machinery and products of your business. Talk, ask, look and listen—be in touch with your entire organization. When there's trouble, you'll know it on the day it happens, or only one day later; not when a bad quarterly report shows up.

But even after you have created swift and digestible data input—your Monday morning "film" —it is important to remember as a quarterback not to *overcritique* yourself. Overanalyzing and second-guessing yourself like Knute Rockne's barber can become dangerous and counterproductive if carried to extremes. Once you've seen the films and absorbed the lessons, it is time to indulge in some creative forgetting and get back onto the playing field as if you had never really lost. Scuff your knuckles and bang your shins. The film is just a film; the game is the real thing. Monday lasts for one day only.

FACT: *You don't know whether a play works until you run it—get into the arena and play your game. No good decision was ever made in a swivel chair.*

14.

MYTH: *One-Sided Deals Leave You Sitting Pretty*

"They'll fire you for losing before they'll fire you for cheating." This is a truism that many fans believe about sports: winning is so important that it excuses anything. Unfortunately, it is sometimes true. Even worse, this ethic has now all too often been carried over into the world of business, where it can do a great deal more harm than on the playing field.

Cheating and lying have become acceptable parts of doing business in America. Usually it does not go so far as someone's actually committing a crime, but takes the form of trying to screw people with one-sided deals.

Hollywood is famous for one-sided deals. When someone wants to screw you in the film world, you know what they will say to you? "Trust me!" It's just accepted in Hollywood that the other guys want to screw you, and if you're not shrewd enough to screw them back, then too bad for you. In fact, there's an accounting firm in New York whose sole job is to audit television shows and film productions so that people who own a part of them make sure they're not getting screwed.

It happens in other businesses, too. The people who do this think it's great to screw someone because it makes them shrewder or smarter than the other person. What they don't realize is that each time they do it, they're cutting off one more finger. Sometimes they get short-term gains out of it, but in the long term, they won't get substance and growth from that deal. Business is more than just next year.

It happens in professional football, too. There are general managers of teams that take an athlete or his agent and really think if they can screw him and give him less than the market price around the league, they've done yeoman's service.

In making deals, you buy and sell a lot. I don't want to steal from somebody. I may want to come back and make a deal with you tomorrow, or maybe next year. I'm going to do my best to look at the contract from both sides and make a fair, upright, handshake deal with you. I want to make out and I want *you* to make out.

There are different kinds of deals, of course.

Sometimes you're dealing for long-term gains; other times for more cash into your company right now. But on down the road after the deal is made, we all determine whether the other guy tried to screw us. When I make a deal with somebody, I want him to be able to look at it five years from now and say, "Tarkenton made a fair deal with me."

There are two things involved here. One, the ethics. Two, it's good business. If I've been honest and tried to make a fair deal and look at it from both sides so you can come out and I can come out, you're going to deal with me again, aren't you? But if you find that I'm a son of a bitch who made a one-sided deal with you where I made out and you lost your ass, you're not going to deal with me again. And you shouldn't.

Maybe what it all comes down to is trust. I think we need to reestablish trust in our business dealings by bringing honesty and candor to our negotiations. You can't bullshit or try to trick the other guy. Your negotiating partner is probably talking not only with you but with some competition as well. Probably both of you are offering good products at relatively similar prices. That customer is finally going to buy from the person he trusts the most.

You establish trust with candor and honesty and by not using gimmicks or tricks. You can't be deceptive and win consistently. Sometimes you've seen someone start at square one and fly high right away. You say, "Shit, boy, look at them!" And you know that company or person is using dirty tricks and unethical tactics and that some things may not be completely honorable. You get tempted to say, "God, maybe that's the way to do it, because look how well they're doing."

But most of the people I've seen taking off like that come down burning. Look at John DeLorean. He had everybody, including the whole British government, persuaded to invest in a company that soon went bankrupt. Jake Butcher, developer of the 1982 World's Fair, had his banking empire collapse around him. David Begelman, the movie mogul who got hot at the top, was convicted of embezzling funds from Columbia Pictures.

One of the best ways to rebuild honesty and trust in your corporate life is to bring emotion back into business. We need some entrepreneurial passion in the boardroom that makes people stand in their chairs and shout with excitement about some new product they have developed. I don't generally believe that cheerleading is the secret to business success, but I do believe we need a strong *emotional commitment* to our products and our services. That is the first way to develop trust in the marketplace.

An emotional commitment to my own business served me well recently when I realized that Exxon, the petroleum giant, was going to renege on a deal with me. I entered their conference room, opened my bag of chewing tobacco, spat into a porcelain coffee cup and said, "Well, I see the largest corporation in the world is here with their lawyers, and one of the biggest ad agencies in the world is here with its lawyers— and I'm here. Alone. Gentlemen, that's a fair fight."

The difference was that I was fighting for *my* money and they were fighting for Exxon's. Because I'm not an unbending soul, I offered to let them out of the deal and settle for roughly six times their original offer. Whereupon I left for California, where I later got the news that the oil company had accepted. They realized I had a strong emotional commitment to my business and to my reputation—and that I wasn't afraid to show it and fight for it.

People have to know you are not bullshitting them. When I told my teammates on the Vikings that I wanted their input in calling the offensive plays, they had to know I meant it. They would see right through me immediately if I only talked about it but did not carry it out. That kind of one-sided deal would have swiftly undermined my leadership.

The point of this chapter is: *You don't want to screw the guy you're negotiating with.* Business is always a two-way street, and if you dirty up one side of it, you're not going to be able to tread that way again when the time comes. If you make deals that are good for you but no good for the other guy, you're going to win for a short period, but somewhere down the line

those *one-sided deals will come back to haunt
you.*

FACT: *One-sided deals will come back to
haunt you; therefore, don't sell—let
the client buy.*

15.

MYTH: *A Smart Leader Has All the Answers*

I can get people to tell me anything. One time I was sitting with John Davidson, my co-host on "That's Incredible." We were having lunch in a Hollywood restaurant when we fell into conversation with two women at the next table. Within just a few minutes I had them telling us the most private details of their personal lives.

Afterwards, John said, "That was incredible!" (No connection to the show.)

I said, "But John, didn't you notice what *you* said? You told us everything about yourself, too. You were saying things so private that most people pay a psychiatrist good money to listen to them."

John was amazed. But he had learned something about me: I am insatiably curious. The more important point was that we both recognized something deeply ingrained in human nature: *people love to talk about themselves.*

When I was with the Minnesota Vikings, they used to kid me about all the questions I asked. I don't mean questions about throwing footballs or next week's game. I mean questions around the front office—about trades, gate receipts, travel costs; about the whole business of running a football franchise.

Our general manager, Mike Lynn, once told a reporter, "Fran wanted to know all about me and my business. He made suggestions on trades and told me how much people should be paid. It was outlandish. He was like an owner."

Maybe it *was* outlandish, but Mike never refused to talk to me. In fact, I think he *loved* explaining the ins and outs of the football business to me. I did not know it then, but this would help me a lot in my later business life.

What I did know then was to ask questions. I was always a successful athlete, yet I always had a healthy respect for my ignorance of a lot of other things in life. I was no A-plus student in high school or college, though I was no dummy either. That's why I have always asked a lot of questions. I recognized that books and lectures were not going to be the path to wisdom for the preacher's boy. It was going to be through people.

All the knowledge and wisdom in the books came through people. Somebody had to write those words. And it is a great deal more fun to get the information directly from the source than secondhand through the person's writings. But some of the smartest people I have learned from couldn't even write their way out of a traffic ticket. Their wisdom came from experience, and *they are always willing to share it—if you ask.*

The man who taught me the importance of asking questions was Roger Milliken, third-generation owner and chairman of Milliken & Company of Spartanburg, South Carolina. Mr. Milliken became my first client when I went into the behavior-management business in 1971. He *made* our business, and I'll never forget it.

Mr. Milliken is a very low-key man. His family has owned the business for 100 years and made it into perhaps the best textile company in the world. Mr. Milliken—that's what I still call him—is one of the world's wealthiest men, but you'd never know it. He is the kind of guy who can walk through his sixty plants and know the loom fixers and yarn spinners by their first names.

But at this time, Milliken & Company was suffering a turnover problem with its personnel. And Roger Milliken was willing to listen to this young quarterback starting up a new business.

I'll never forget sitting in his office that day. I felt like a Little League coach trying to counsel Vince Lombardi. Mr. Milliken said to me, "Fran, here's the problem and it's killing us. What do you think you can do?" He sat there and listened to me outline our ideas. When I finished, he said, "I'm going to give you a chance. I'm going to put you in our Armitage plant over on Interstate 85."

What impressed me the most was that a man running a multibillion-dollar business, surrounded with all kinds of knowledge and expertise, was willing to listen to a guy he had just met—to see if he might have a good idea. Apparently I did, because he later sent us into more than fifty of his plants.

One time I found myself in a golf tournament sponsored by United Airlines for some of the corporate leaders of America. Harry Gray of United Technologies was there, and so were Jimmy Robinson, the chairman of American Express, Jack Handly, the chairman of Monsanto, Charlie Brown, the chairman of AT&T, and a lot of others.

On the plane out to the West Coast, I spotted Gen. William Westmoreland a few seats behind me. He was then president of the Citadel and had also been invited to the tournament. After the takeoff, I went back and asked if I could talk with him for a few minutes. We spent the next five hours discussing wars and battles and military policy. It was a better education than I could have gotten in a year at West Point.

One day during the tournament, I went up to Harry Gray and said, "Could I have lunch with you, Mr. Gray?"

He said, "Call me Harry." While we were having lunch, Jimmy Robinson came by. I already knew Jimmy, so I introduced him to Harry Gray and we ate together. They launched into a discussion of mergers and takeovers. Gray had a reputation as a successful acquirer of companies while Jimmy Robinson had just had the acquisition of McGraw-Hill fall apart on him. I learned more about the problems of large business mergers in our country from these two men in two hours over lunch than they teach in two years at the Harvard Business School.

I knew nothing about mergers when I went in and a lot when I came out—though I did not specifically need the information. But it came in awfully handy several years later when I was invited into a consortium of Atlanta investors who came close to buying the Pabst Brewing Company. As it turned out, our deal fell through, but that does not mean I won't someday be in another situation where that lunchtime wisdom will help me in business.

But this does not make any difference; you can learn something from anyone. At all levels, in every arena, there are people who know things you don't.

Peter Grace once surprised a journalist who had come to interview him by first interviewing the reporter. When the journalist finally had a chance to remind Peter that he had come to ask the questions, not the other way around, Peter replied, "Of course, but I learn things by talking to as many people as I can."

That's my policy, too.

I pick people's brains wherever I meet them: on airplanes, at airports, in coffee shops. Recently I was playing golf with a local Pontiac dealer. You know what I started out asking him? "Tell me about Henry Ford and the way the American car business started." After we had talked about that for a while, he mentioned that he had just added Isuzu to his car line, so I said, "Tell me about the Japanese and how they are building cars." He didn't know why I was asking all these questions, but he was glad to answer them. *People love to talk about themselves and their work.*

I try never to forget the lesson Roger Milliken taught me so many years ago: *You're never too big or too smart to learn from anyone.* And from Harry Gray I learned: "Don't just go fishing when you retire. Go hunting." Keep asking questions, listening to answers, building on your own ideas.

But you don't have to have access to the top minds in American business to get valuable information. Often, all you need to know is how to use the information at hand. Ironically most companies have available to them too much information rather than too little, yet they seldom put it to good use. The advent of the microcomputer and productivity tools for data processing now gives us the opportunity to put all the reams of paper into a concentrated format so that we can have whatever information we need in a form we can use.

Don't underestimate the wealth of information available to you from your data processing people once you learn to communicate with them. At Tarkenton Productivity Group we concentrate on increased productivity through the effective management of information. A good data processing department helps improve productivity throughout a business organization.

FACT: *Always ask, always listen.*

16.

MYTH: *Always Play As if You Are Ahead*

The games I lost were always the ones I thought I had won. Thinking you are ahead, in business or in football, is a sure way to fall behind. It has been my lucky experience that whenever I think I've mastered something, I proceed to get my ass kicked. That's why it is important always to play the games of business and sports as if you are behind.

I learned this lesson in embarrassing and no uncertain terms during my second year in professional football. Our fledgling Vikings expansion team had trounced the mighty Chicago Bears in the previous season opener at Memorial Stadium in Bloomington, Minnesota. Then our hot young team went out and promptly lost its next six games with Mr. Perfect at quarterback. We went into too many games thinking we already had them won—and so we lost.

One game the following season taught me the importance of never playing as if you are ahead, even when you *are*. We were playing the Bears at Soldiers Field in Chicago. Going into the final minutes of the game, we were leading by two points and had possession of the ball deep in our own territory. All I had to do was run down the clock and go home with a victory over the mighty Monsters of the Midway. I could have called a quarterback sneak and fallen on the ground, but instead I called an off-tackle run for fullback Doug Mayberry.

No sooner had Mayberry plunged into the line than I saw black Chicago shirts diving into a pile of bodies on the ground. Then the umpire began signaling that the Bears had recovered a fumble! We had lost possession of the ball in our own territory, and now Chicago's place-kicking team was coming onto the field! I stood on the sidelines with my mouth open about 10 feet while Papa Bear Halas's boys calmly won the game with a field goal as the clock ran down. I had played as if I was ahead and lost the game! I had gotten sloppy and called a hand-off when I should have eaten the ball and fallen on the ground. By giving the ball to my fullback, I was setting him up for the remote *chance of failure*. I had not taken the ultimate precaution to ensure victory.

I was acting like the businessman who thinks a deal is done before it's signed, sealed and the check is delivered (*and* has cleared the bank). Any "done" deal that comes undone wasn't really a done deal; it was an almost-done deal, just as my game against the Bears was "almost" won. There is, of course, no such thing as almost winning—except in the Olympics, where you can come in second, or—as some wag has said—in medical school, where they call even the last-place finisher "Doctor." But in football and in business deals, old Yogi Berra taught us all a great lesson when he said: "The game ain't over until it's over."

The closer you are to victory—we were only thirty seconds away that day in Chicago—the more imperative it becomes to attend to every detail of winning. I have seen big business deals fall apart when someone got careless and sloppy at the contract-signing stage because he was so elated over the success of the basic negotiations. We had *basically* already won that game in Chicago—until the quarterback got elated and sloppy in the final seconds. We assume victory. Most of my mistakes are ones of assumption rather than knowledge or logic.

If you play not to lose, you'll lose. The company that just tries to *hold* its position in the market will soon be passed. Playing to win means always playing as if you are behind—and struggling for perfection. Perfection means covering every detail of victory—even if it means falling on the ground with the football. There is nothing like the prospect of being hanged to concentrate the mind—as Dr. Samuel Johnson pointed out. You'll cover every detail more carefully if you play as though you're running third in a marathon with 3 miles to go.

Some managers believe that if they concentrate on the big picture, the details will take care of themselves. But most errors in business, I have found, are mistakes of assumption rather than logic. In business and in sports, *it's the little things that beat you.*

FACT: *There's nothing like a hanging to concentrate the mind—always play as if you were losing.*

17.

MYTH: *Hard Work Ensures Success*

How many times has your subconscious lectured you on the virtues of keeping farmer's hours and performing back-breaking toil just as you sat down to watch some weekend sports on television? I've heard that voice too, and sometimes I listened to it, just because people I admired were saying the same thing. Harry Gray spends so much time on the job that his employees say, "Harry thinks a vacation is coming to work in a sports jacket."

But hard work and endless hours are not necessarily a direct route to success. This is one area where athletes have often been smarter than their business counterparts with their M.B.A.'s and pressed silk ties. How well do you think your favorite pro football team would play on Sunday if it went out and exhausted itself on Saturday? In pro football, you use Mondays for films and analysis of the previous game; Tuesday as your day off; and Wednesdays, Thursdays and Fridays for hard workouts.

But Saturday is always fun day—the day when you bring your kids to practice and you work out in your shorts. Saturday is the day to prepare your *mind, not your body.* Officially you prepare your mind by going over the game plan and running through the plays, discussing once again what to expect from the next day's opponent. *Unofficially* you prepare your mind by simple relaxation. Saturday is meant for making cracks and pulling pranks—the things that help gel the team into a single working spirit for the game ahead.

Old Casey Stengel, repository of half the baseball wisdom in the history of the game (Yogi Berra owns the other half), had a similar way of getting his ball players up for their games. According to writer Maury Allen, he was "a tremendous organizer, determined that his players would be moving at all times." His players would warm up on calisthenics, work in the field, take laps around the park, be in constant motion until their hitting turn came. They wouldn't lounge around at the batting cage, but neither would they work out so thoroughly they'd already played a whole game in their minds. This was Casey's way of keeping everybody loose *and* limber for the big games.

In business, it's crucial to keep your mind primed for opportunities, to stay aware of changes going on around you. You can't do this well when you're constantly drained by nine-to-nine shifts. Your best ideas may come when you're on the slopes or in a game of touch football.

Even Jack Welch, the young, hard-driving chairman of General Electric, knows that some time off can do wonders for his creative mind. Jack works about forty-two hours per minute, but he also knows how to play hard. If he's racing around to G.E. plants all over the country, he often suddenly stops off somewhere in Colorado so he can "ski like hell for four or five days."

If you're working all the time, you're working against yourself. You're not being your most productive.

Once I was visiting with a leading textile company in South Carolina. One of the vice-presidents invited me for a drink after work, so I came by his office about five-thirty and asked if he was ready. He looked at me as if I were a crazy man.

"Nobody leaves before seven o'clock," he said.

"Why?" I asked. "Do you have more work to do?"

"No, we just all stay until seven. That's when the boss leaves."

If you're staying around your office with no real work to do just because the boss is there, you're not working productively. Part of productivity is rest, recreation and renewal. If you're coming in on Saturdays not out of necessity but out of inefficiency, boredom or guilt, you're not working productively. You may think you're working hard, but *you're not working smart.* That would be about as productive as forcing the Minnesota Vikings into a full-dress, hard-tackle workout on the Saturday before a game.

Your goal as a productive businessman should not be to work harder, but to work smarter. I think even Harry Gray would agree with that.

My personal style is to build recreation right into my schedule every week. If you are working all the time, you're actually *wasting* company time. You serve your job better by allowing your mind to leave work so you can come back fresh and see problems with new insight, determination and a stronger fighting spirit. Some of my most creative work is done when I'm sitting still—often in airplanes. One weekend I treated myself to a few days off in Lake Tahoe, California. I relaxed, but I kept limber. I left the hotel Jacuzzi and the golf course with a notebook full of new ideas for my company. Some of them I know would have even beaten old Casey.

FACT: *Don't work harder, work* limber.

18.

MYTH: *To Come Out Ahead, Beware the Competition*

Beware the enemy? Concentrate on the 240-pound linebacker blitzing through the line right toward you? Never! A quarterback has to concentrate on putting the ball into the receiver's hands. If I spent all my time worrying about the defense chasing me around, I would never throw the pass.

In business, the reality is: *Beware the customer!* He's your toughest critic, whose anger or satisfaction can make or break you. The great Lew Lehr of 3M says that the people you must outdo are your customers: "To persuade effectively, you must have more imagination than your audience."

In football, you learn through films what to

expect every Sunday from your adversary—the opposing team's defense. You scout your adversary for speed, strength, endurance and his love of points-at-any-cost—even at the cost of your intact body. But business is an offensive sport—there really is no defense, nobody you can send out to crush your competition for you. So the best thing to do is concentrate on your own offense.

Yet, most businessmen I know think too defensively. They become preoccupied with their competition. They're always thinking, What are they doing over there at Company B? Or, What's the guy in the next office doing that I'm not? Is he buddying up to the boss? What has he got planned? Are they trying to steal my pattern?

What does this do? It gives the advantage to the other guy. You start to play *his* game. You can become so focused on the other guy that you turn paranoid and spend all your time thinking about the competition when you should be thinking about yourself and your own team, about developing that new product, finalizing your new strategies or chasing down accounts—and the other offensive tactics that will help your company grow.

It is a big mistake to spend too much time worrying about *them* and not enough concentrating on *us*.

The best businessmen say, "Damn the torpedoes, full-speed ahead. We're going to find out what the competition has by discovering who and where our customer is." They concentrate on the marketplace, on the customer and on their own performance, not on the competition. A man who is one of the greatest quarterbacks business has seen is G.E.'s Jack Welch. His philosophy is: "Don't sit and worry about the risk to you. Go do it. It'll work out. Make it work out."

It's like the strategy that Delta Air Lines has. After all, they don't fly the competition, they fly customers. Delta chairman David C. Garrett, Jr., once said, "We have two rules about our passengers. One: The passenger is always right. Two: If you're in doubt, go back and refer to rule number one." Or, follow the lead of Fred Smith, the genius founder of Federal Express. He allows everybody—all his competition—to observe his technology, his operations, his company's culture. While they're concentrating on him, he's walking away with more and more of their customers.

FACT: *Ignore the competition; love the customer.*

19.

MYTH: *Second Always Finishes Behind First*

Nobody wants to be second. But why not?

A winner is *supposed* to come in second. If you do everything I've described in this book: if you involve your players, create teamwork, deliver feedback and reinforcement, show your people that you care and—eureka!—that puts you second and puts your people, concerns and company first.

One of the most important lessons I had to learn was that a victory should not necessarily make you a winner. If you've done well, it's because you've helped others to win. You may be the best player on your tennis courts right now—or the hottest salesman in the company for one month—but you'll keep that lead only when you put other things first.

Of course, you couldn't have told that to a certain 21-year-old rookie quarterback of the Minnesota Vikings on a certain Sunday afternoon back in 1961. I had been chosen as a third-round draft pick by this lowly expansion team, but they were in the National Football League and that is where I wanted to play. We were mostly castoffs from other clubs—and rookies right out of college, like me. But our first regular-season game was to be against the mighty Chicago Bears, the Monsters of the Midway. The Bears had earned that nickname. They were the oldest team in professional football, started by their coach and owner, the late George "Papa Bear" Halas. It was Halas who practically started the National Football League. It should not surprise you that we Vikings were something like 24-point underdogs that day. We had just gone through a five-game exhibition season with a record of no wins and five losses. The year before, another expansion team, the Dallas Cowboys, had gone to the post twelve times and lost eleven games and tied one. So nobody thought Minnesota had a chance against Chicago. When the teams were announced at the beginning of the game, our hometown crowd cheered more for the Bears than for us. After all, they had been watching Chicago on television for years. They didn't even know our names.

Our fresh-baked Vikings team could have

sat in that locker room that Sunday afternoon and written off that game. Who were we to take on the Chicago Bears? History wasn't on our side. Our exhibition record wasn't on our side. We could have thought of every reason in the world why we couldn't win, and nobody expected us to.

But the beauty and the naiveté of sport is that we forty guys were dumb enough and naive enough to think that *we had a chance to win!* How could we think such a thing, when even Howard Cosell said we couldn't win? How could we defy *his* indisputable logic? We did not necessarily think we *would* win, but we thought we *could* win.

I don't know about you, but I have never succeeded in doing anything when I didn't think I *could*, where I felt there was a 100-percent "no chance." But when I thought I *could*, at least I had some chance, no matter what the odds.

So we went out and played that day. We played those old Monsters of the Midway and we didn't just beat them, we blew them away. Final score: 38–13.

The little 21-year-old kid from Georgia was at quarterback that day. My memory is a little fuzzy now, but I think I completed seventeen of twenty-one passes with no interceptions for 238½ yards for three touchdowns and ran for another.

You can imagine how I felt that day when I walked off the field. All of a sudden my teammates had me up on their shoulders. All 47,000 people in Memorial Stadium were up on their feet yelling and screaming. Somehow they had now learned my name.

And all of a sudden this little guy with his derby hat and glasses comes pushing through the crowd and pokes his hand up to me and says, "Kid, that's the greatest rookie performance I've ever seen in the history of this League." That man was George Halas.

By now I was thinking, "Wow, Mama, you were right! You always said I was special from the day I was born. I am! They love me!"

I said to myself, "Unitas and Tittle and Baugh, you all were my heroes. I planned to be great sometime, but look what I've done on the first day! Move over!"

I thought, "This is easy! I have made it! *I have arrived!* Where do I go from here?"

I went into that locker room after the game, and my teammates were telling the press what a great leader I was. I heard one of my coaches tell a sportswriter that I was perfection. And I thought he was absolutely right-on, brother!

Well, I walked out of the locker room that day, and there was my little Georgia-peach wife, and I said to her, "Honey, do you realize how many truly great quarterbacks there are in the world today?"

And she said, "One fewer than you think."

My wife obviously knew something that I didn't, because our wonderful team promptly went out and lost our next six games in a row with Mr. Perfect at quarterback. That was the last time in my pro career that I ever thought that I had *arrived*. I learned that the minute you think you've arrived is the moment you'll start to lose. Not just because *there is no such thing as arriving*, but because once you feel you're indispensable, you start becoming blind to the essentials of good business—teamwork, feedback, reinforcement. The true winner doesn't think he has beat the world after his first good Sunday. He doesn't suddenly think God believes in *him*. As a winner, you should come to consider winning an everyday proposition, not a divine gift for you alone.

Winning is indeed an everyday proposition—it must be earned all over again, every time you play the game.

Learn scorekeeping, feedback and reinforcement. Practice teamwork, involvement and sharing. Drop the ways of the macho manager and of trying to live by the big play. Stop, look, listen and learn. Never feel you've come in first just because you won. "An excellent team is a group of people that play better than their parts," said John Madden, who once coached the Raiders.

But what makes it all work for you on a continuing basis is the search for better ways to live and work and play. Remember that no matter how great your victory today, tomorrow is a new game with new plays and new opponents. You're a winner if you get into the arena and play—the stakes are high, but the rewards are great. What makes it exciting and worth the risk is the wonderful, unending uncertainty of how the game will go, for the clock never stops and the score can always change tomorrow.

FACT: *A winner is supposed to come in second.*

TARK'S TRUTHS

1. When all is said and done, more is said than done. *Make it happen!*

2. A winning performance always beats a winning attitude. Give me action, not motivation.

3. Performance is not a function of salary; salary is a function of performance.

4. Give your people a scoreboard: They need to know whether they are winning or losing.

5. People don't want praise so much as attention—*you gotta care!*

6. Don't be afraid of the boss—he needs you too.

7. No good advice has ever been given at the top of one's lungs.

8. The good news: It's okay to lose.

9. Quitting is not the opposite of winning—it's part of winning.

10. Beware the big play: The 80-yard drive is better than the 80-yard pass.

11. It takes a team to make a superstar.

12. *You*, not your barber, are the best Monday-morning quarterback.

13. You don't know whether a play works until you run it—get into the arena and play your game. No good decision was ever made in a swivel chair.

14. One-sided deals will come back to haunt you; therefore, don't sell—let the client buy.

15. Always ask, always listen.

16. There's nothing like a hanging to concentrate the mind—always play as if you were losing.

17. Don't work harder, work *limber*.

18. Ignore the competition; love the customer.

19. A winner is supposed to come in second.

ABOUT THE AUTHOR

Fran Tarkenton is familiar to millions of people, not just to those who remember his football days with the New York Giants and the Minnesota Vikings. He is now a co-host of the television show "That's Incredible." In addition, he is a business consultant to major firms and runs his own highly successful business, Tarkenton Productivity Group, Inc., in Atlanta.

SPECIAL
MONEY SAVING
OFFER

Now you can have an up-to-date listing of Bantam's hundreds of titles plus take advantage of our unique and exciting bonus book offer. A special offer which gives you the opportunity to purchase a Bantam book for only 50¢. Here's how!

By ordering any five books at the regular price per order, you can also choose any other single book listed (up to a $4.95 value) for just 50¢. Some restrictions do apply, but for further details why not send for Bantam's listing of titles today!

Just send us your name and address plus 50¢ to defray the postage and handling costs.

BANTAM BOOKS, INC.
Dept. FC, 414 East Golf Road, Des Plaines, Ill 60016

Mr./Mrs./Miss/Ms. _____
(please print)

Address _____

City_____ State_____ Zip_____

FC—3/84

We Deliver!
And So Do These Bestsellers.